Echoes of Silence

By

Bart Seuntjens

Copyright © 2024 by – *Bart Seuntjens* – All Rights Reserved.

It is not legal to reproduce, duplicate, or transmit any part of this document in either electronic means or printed format. Recording of this publication is strictly prohibited.

TABLE OF CONTENTS

DEDICATION i
ACKNOWLEDGMENT ii
ABOUT THE AUTHOR iii
THE ARMPIT 1
THE TRAP 25
OPTIONS 46
THE BARBECUE 61
OPTIONS II 94
LA VIE EN ROSE 114
TOP 5... 151
AN EGG (IS NOT AN EGG) 163
JOYCE 189
THE HUNTERS 223
IN THE ATTIC 242

DEDICATION

To my family, friends, and Raquel—thank you for providing endless material for this book, even though you had no idea I was writing it! Here's to accidentally becoming muses.

ACKNOWLEDGMENT

Thank you to the journey that shaped this book—the life that handed me not just sunshine but storms, not just answers but endless mysteries. To my naïveté, imagination, and unwavering positivity, you helped me dream big and stay strong. I owe you everything.

ABOUT THE AUTHOR

Bart Seuntjens, is a Dutch consultant living in Belgium for more than 30 years. He is happily married to his Spanish wife, Raquel, and they raise 5 kids together and have 2 dogs (Bart still wonders 'Why?'). Apart from being a professional consultant, he shares lots of interest in (Spanish) wine, photography, nature and biking.

THE ARMPIT

"What were the first symptoms?" The man looked at me intently in his white doctor's outfit. He was in his early 30s, slightly nervous, shuffling in his seat. "Did you have extra stress at that time, or were there specific issues in your professional and/or private life?" Her sharply ironed, flawless white apron, under which I noticed a blue lace slip, was tight around her body. As she introduced herself, Olga might have come from the Eastern Bloc, given her appearance and name, but she spoke my language fluently. Suddenly, it became clear to me. Julie had voluntarily admitted me to a facility. It had come to this. My beloved wife had betrayed me, reached out to a 'white coat clinic' for mentally unstable and disturbed individuals, and cleverly sold it to me under the guise of a visit to a 'wellness center.' I honestly had respect and admiration for her inventiveness. I looked at the result in the mirror with a face contorted with pain. Both arms raised and hands on the neck. They looked like two sliced grapefruits. My physical reality.

The very first time, John had rather clumsily drawn my attention to it. In the introductory meeting with Spenser's CEO, we reviewed the possibilities and potential solutions we had in store to streamline their Human Resources department. I listened to Eric Spenser's account but couldn't keep my attention on it. I usually went through the first meeting on autopilot, with the trends and tendencies I casually presented being enough to gain credibility and enter a sales process. Not today. The total inability to stay focused created a particularly uncomfortable feeling that I tried to hide through my non-verbal behavior and body language. I leaned back casually and put my hands on my neck, pretending to listen. That was the moment I saw John's gaze freeze on me. My first reflex was that elements mentioned in the discussion now required an appropriate intervention based on my expertise in the HR domain. I quickly tried to recall Spenser's spoken words to discern a common thread so I could skillfully intervene. But there was nothing, and nothing came to mind. John still looked at me, now with his eyes rolled upwards, while Eric continued his speech, which completely passed me. And I was increasingly curious about the signals John was sending, which clearly concerned me and which I couldn't decipher. HR manager Peter Stills joined the discussion by opening his mouth, and Eric's meaningless words were interspersed with Peter's and John's right arm lightly FLAPPING MOVEMENTS. It was a ridiculous sight, especially since, in the same rhythm, now, the index finger of his left hand pointed to his raised right arm. How long would it take for Eric or Peter to ask what was wrong with John? No need to worry about that since both gentlemen were now engaged in an intensive discussion where Eric seemed to get more and more agitated. John had slumped wearily in his chair with his left index finger resting conspicuously on the armpit of his immaculately pink shirt. At that moment, I felt a drop running down the inside of my right arm along the side of my body. I glanced at my shirt. A giant dark blue circle had spread from the armpit over my light blue shirt. Embarrassing.

After the meeting, I rushed to the toilet to thoroughly dry my armpit with a small towel. It was only my right armpit, my left one was fine. Then, I contorted myself in all sorts of ways to catch the hot air from the hand dryer with my armpit. As I bent under the hand dryer, John unexpectedly entered the toilet. "Boy, in the future, keep your blazer on. This wasn't professional," said John as I heard his zipper open. I made myself scarce.

Since then, it has been downhill. That is to say, from that particular meeting onwards, I was confronted daily, truly daily, with the emphatic existence of my armpit and the presence of particularly active sweat glands in the hollow under my right arm. From the moment I showered, first applied my deodorant stick and then my deodorant spray, and put on my white T-shirt, it started to feel damp and moist under my right armpit. There was no remedy for it. A stinking fungus emitting its toxic juices unchecked, an erupted sweat volcano spewing endless amounts of perspiration lava. By around 10 o'clock, I was sitting with a soaked shirt and undershirt and could do nothing but either press my right arm tightly against my body or keep my blazer on. Usually, I did both. At first, I just felt extremely uncomfortable, but over time, I began to worry. What caused this waterfall of perspiration? Was it anxiety sweat of which I was not yet aware? Did I have an incredibly scary disease? Had the sweat glands of my left armpit moved to the right armpit without my knowledge to be joined by all the sweat glands of my entire body and end up in an unrestrained party explosion. Many questions arose with the dark, ever-growing circles in my shirt. The sweating continued while I diligently searched for answers regarding the underlying cause and solutions to limit the visible impact on my shirts. I became obsessed with this relatively small area of my body, resulting in moments when I felt like I was transforming into one big dark armpit where the forest of pubic hair generated seas of sweat. Eventually, the water literally ran from the side of my upper body up my back towards my buttocks.

The search for effective solutions demanded a lot of my creativity. It quickly became clear that the average deodorant had no impact whatsoever. Since Julie washed my shirts and I expected questions due to the increased humidity in my shirts, I decided to come clean. Julie showed a lot of understanding, urged me to see a psychologist urgently, and even took the initiative to stock up on entire assortments of deodorants. Sticks, rollers, creams, sprays; my sink was full of them, and one by one, and later, in all sorts of combinations, they found their way to my armpit. Time and time again, the disappointment was immense. Over time, I realized that the misery only grew because, in addition to a constant flow of sweat, I was now also incurring costs, and dubious-looking brown stains were forming in my shirts and T-shirts, possibly caused by the various exotic deodorant cocktails. The stains turned out to be extremely stubborn, resulting in me being unable to wear certain clothes anymore. Especially the so-called anti-perspirant deodorants I got from the pharmacy were disastrous. They cost three times as much as supermarket products, felt extremely unpleasantly sticky, and guaranteed a greasy broth under the arm within the hour. In addition to extensively testing and unlimitedly failing with the various deodorant products, I also started to search for ways to absorb the sweat so that it didn't always lead to visible spots around my armpit. 'Around my armpit,' because by now, the circles had a diameter of about 40 centimeters. It was truly going from bad to worse. My attempts to prevent soaking started with placing handkerchiefs under the right armpit. When I drove to work, I then set the air conditioning to maximum volume at a temperature of 19°C, directed the air vents as best as possible to my right upper arm, and rested it on the headrest of the passenger seat. This action allowed me to keep it dry for about 3 hours from the time I left home. To extend this, I replaced the handkerchief every 2 hours. However, most of the time, I had to acknowledge, upon changing the second handkerchief, that the damage had been done. So, I resorted to other drastic measures. I switched to restaurant napkins. Since I regularly ate at such establishments, I began accumulating a collection of towels that Julie no longer recognized. But nothing helped. The absorption rate of the various fibers in any form was no match for the activity, intensity, and humidity of my armpit.

I often lay awake at night, racking my brain over the physical problem I had been confronted with lately. While I was obsessed daily with the issue of my wet armpit, and especially how to prevent the visible damage, or at least postpone it for as long as possible (I didn't get past 1:30 PM. usually before, but at the latest at that time it became visibly damp), it was especially during the nocturnal hours that I pondered what the underlying real problem of that endless flow of bodily fluids was. It must be related to my professional career because as soon as I came home, my armpit became passive, the river of sweat stopped, and a dry period followed. One night, everything suddenly seemed clear to me. Although the sex with Julie had been particularly satisfying and exhausting, I couldn't fall asleep, lay on my back, and let the saga of the 'eternally weeping armpit' pass before me from the beginning to the current chapter. The meeting with John and Spensers had taken place two weeks earlier. Upon reflection, it was only the second day after my most disastrous Easter vacation. During that leave, I was constantly interrupted for work, and I had been extremely irritated. My potential cynicism and frustration had occasionally surfaced, but always just before the leave. To throw some jabs, knowing that I would be lounging in a beach chair with sun and drinks within reach, sufficiently rested to dive back into work after the vacation. This year, I'm back from vacation. It seems like the climb up the Cynicism Mountain is only halfway there, with an increasingly lower irritation threshold. Was it because a few weeks earlier, it became apparent that the smallest 'window of opportunity' for me was enough to make the difference between delightful, carefree sex and guaranteeing offspring? Was it because I was confronted with the awareness that I was currently producing children faster than projects? I was 38, probably according to the norm, an extremely successful Director at Value Creators Inc., who had so far had a lightning-fast career and a glorious future ahead.

I had never planned my professional life, and my career at Value Creators Inc. had actually just happened to me. Ironically, the 'accidental career takeover' occurred within a company where careers could mainly be made and survived by ambitious, know-it-all, and selfish individuals addicted to their work. OK, Julie regularly accused me of being know-it-all and narcissistic, but that was different. If only I were addicted to my work, I thought.

Damn, maybe that was it. Had I become unknowingly addicted to my work? Had I turned into that workaholic I always thought I recognized in others? Had I unconsciously undergone a development that I had always thought, or rather, loudly proclaimed, would never happen to me. And was my pouring armpit a symptom of going cold turkey? Was that drenched sponge under my right arm a wake-up call?

Julie withdrew her support for me, partly because I refused to see a psychologist and partly because she wasn't on board with a new proposal of mine that apparently didn't appeal to her. After the tissues and the towels, I felt I had to resort to more drastic, invasive measures. Applying or stitching chamois into my shirts seemed like the only 'way to go.' Since Julie thought I was crazy and wanted no part in sewing chamois into shirts, I had to find help elsewhere. In moments like these, you realize there's only one woman in your life you can truly rely on.

My mother was initially delighted, surprised, and extremely worried when she saw me standing there with a fully loaded weekend bag that Saturday morning. "Tell me it's not true," she said, tears welling up in her eyes. In a way, she sounded more hopeful than shocked. You truly can't keep anything hidden from your own mother, I thought, looking at my right armpit. But there was nothing to see. It was Saturday, and I was relaxed. It took me a moment to realize what she suspected. In fact, I was starting to worry now because she gave me the impression that she had always expected this and that it was just a matter of time. Moreover, when I broached the subject of my armpits with appropriate embarrassment, she seemed more upset by the fact that my marriage was still holding up than by the drama of my weeping armpit. Mothers.

A few years ago, I had already set my parents on a certain track, so my mother's reaction wasn't entirely unexpected now. Ben had been with us for a few months when all the alarm bells in my system started ringing, and both the mechanisms of a delayed (or perhaps extended) puberty and those of an early midlife crisis joined forces against my good intentions as the (happy?) new father of little Ben, conceived with the woman of my life, the resident child psychiatrist. Just as Ben nowadays suffered from a chronic lack of resistance and an immune system prone to colds and infections, I seemed to be susceptible to every female appearance back then. They seemed to be everywhere I went. In the supermarket, in traffic, on Value Creators Inc.'s projects. They were everywhere. It was like a swarm of mosquitoes.

Where did they suddenly come from? And I must have had something in my blood that attracted them. At first, I was still swatting them away, but soon, I was beyond the stage where they bothered me.

Of course, they had always been there. Life hadn't been the same since the experience with Jane's Pandora's box from a distant past. But it would be absurd to assume that overnight, the number of ripe, challenging women targeting me had increased by a factor of 1000. And yet. I had kept my head above water for years without too much trouble. Sometimes, the waves required a bit more effort, and I had swallowed some water before, but I hadn't gone under. And at other times, it was like floating blissfully in calm waters under a warm sun without any effort. Until...

"Tsunami tsunami came washing over me, tsunami tsunami came washing over me. Can't speak, can't think, won't talk, won't walk.

The doctor tells me that I'm cynical. I tell them that it must be chemical, so what am I doing, girl? Cry into my drink, I disappear."

The Tsunami sung by the Manic Street Preachers on their fantastic 1999 single overwhelmed me like a seaquake should. Neither any seismologist nor the Tsunami Research Centre had warned or at least proactively informed me about the potential threat. I had been a little inattentive when the first slight ripple of the sea level appeared, and I was subsequently sucked in, tossed back and forth, thrown back, and engulfed by the devastating waves. There was no holding back or escaping it. Girl Cry, if only it had stopped at one.

First, there was my own secretary, Inge, who, although she had been working for me for 6 years and, as far as I could remember, had shown no interest in me (or had I shown no interest in her.?) unexpectedly showed interest in her boss's body painting skills after her divorce. While we were going through the agenda for the following week, as we always did on Friday evenings around half past five, and my thoughts were already drifting, the last appointment to verify suddenly led to:

"Umm, Harry. I wanted to ask you for so long, but since Walter and I got divorced, I haven't done any body painting, and I really miss it, so I wanted to ask if you couldn't lend a hand tonight. You once said that despite having two left hands, you're really good with a brush." Apparently, I let my fantasies run a bit too wild while drifting off. "Harry, are you listening?" Two big blue eyes looked at me questioningly. Inge's mini skirt seemed to have retreated a bit at her wearer's words and intentions. Jesus. Why did she have to ask her boss this? What about her social life? And it was Friday, for God's sake, my free evening with Julie. A nice dinner, wine, catching up together in the bath. Inge's mini skirt still seemed a bit threatened and crept up a bit further.

On the other hand, her breasts seemed to subscribe more to the doctrine 'the best defense is a good offense' by coming dangerously close. "Listen, Inge, I appreciate you, and you're a beautiful woman with many qualities (is it impossible to convey this without ambiguity? I wondered as I heard myself). But this doesn't seem like such a good plan. I have a busy weekend, and tonight I have a tête-à-tête with Julie. Undoubtedly, countless other men would be willing to apply a few coats of paint." It was indeed Friday evening, but I found my argumentation extremely weak. Why didn't I just tell her the truth so I could close the door and go straight home?

However, speaking the truth was only a matter of time. "Oh, Inge. What beautiful breasts, and that landscape is quite impressive too, if I may say so myself." I held her right breast in my left hand while putting the finishing touches on the 'I' with my brush. Inge was in ecstasy. Her mini skirt was nowhere to be seen. The coward. The body painting session with Inge was the beginning. Not so much of a body painting career, and I never had anything to do with Inge's mini skirt afterward, but with so many others. I was tossed back and forth and went under heavily.

Agnes came over from Paris to join our team as an HR expert. And I turned out to be a poet who knew his highfalutin literary classics, from Celine to Sartre. Not long after, I met Denise, a 22-year-old British student. It was Friday morning, much too early for the first train to Paris, 6:40 AM Foggy and chilly on the platform. It had become a sort of routine, but I still didn't really get used to it, and this time was different. I waved wistfully and caught a last glimpse of Agnes as the train glided out of the station. Saying goodbye is always difficult. I turned around and bumped into a woman head-on. The impact was so great that I saw stars, my glasses were shattered, and the young woman hit the asphalt of the platform. Through the stars and the shooting pains, I saw her lying there, a wound on her forehead of a disarming face and a slightly strained smile.

I offered to apologize and calm down a bit during our coffee together afterward. It became clear that she was an Erasmus student specializing in a master's in Human Resources. Her thesis she was working on had the pretentious title 'How to Create a High Performing Workforce.' After I told her about my job and role at Value Creators Inc., her eyes sparkled because wasn't I the right person to be interviewed and validate her story? Anyway, one thing led to another, and Denise became a role model for High Performance. And somewhere parallel to British Denise came German Anouk onto the scene. And after German Anouk came to Portuguese Muna. Harry Jones goes international!

Muna was a different story. I was unexpectedly sent to Lisbon for a week to conduct a feasibility study for a Human Resources Shared Service Center. It turned out that in Lisbon, HR was an all-women's affair. The team I had to work with and provide input to was led by Muna, a 29-year-old junior manager with jet-black eyes, a mysterious gaze, and endlessly long legs. Her team also included Inez, Nunu, and Celeste. Before flying in on Thursday evening, I had arranged to have dinner with Muna and her team that same evening, to get acquainted, waste no time, and quickly get up to speed. I was overwhelmed by my table's quantity and quality of female beauty.

The conversation didn't flow fast since I didn't speak Portuguese, but the four ladies spoke English because at Value Creators Inc., didn't we all talk in English? The ladies were constantly chattering away, and I couldn't understand what they were saying, no matter how hard I concentrated. I could only understand Muna, but conducting a job review in these circumstances was impossible. So, I surrendered to Portuguese food, fantastic wine, the live band playing, and my company. During dinner, the ladies also decided that talking didn't make much sense, and communication was limited to eye contact and body language. Inez and Celeste, in particular, were adept at silent but intense interaction with me. It's probably a Portuguese tradition to aid the digestion process, I thought, when around 11 PM, all the tables in the restaurant were pushed aside, and everyone spontaneously started dancing. Inez and Celeste turned out to be the absolute dancing queens of the evening, both making efforts to involve my groin in their act. It wasn't so much that my groin could be convinced. Still, I wasn't keen on publicly displaying my Justin Timberlake moves (it was, after all, my first night!) and having to make a torn choice between these two beauties who were apparently competing for their prey. I retreated to the restaurant's bar, where Muna was waiting for me with a smile and a glass of whiskey.

And after Muna, I lost all sense, was swept further away by each new wave, and never resurfaced.

"Tsunami tsunami came washing over me; tsunami tsunami came washing over me. Can't speak, can't think, won't talk, won't walk."

I don't know, but could it be that men around the age of 35 are confronted with a hormone level that skyrockets like women experience during the third/fourth month of their pregnancy? If that were the case, I would have liked to have heard about it beforehand. And so would Julie, I think. Shortly after our marriage, I became estranged from her and was hardly ever home. When I was home, she complained that I was being distant and seemed far away. If I still loved her, if I still found her attractive. We went to therapy. Perhaps the sessions could have been limited to just me, but under the pretext that 'if there are relational problems within the couple, (at least) two are to blame,' Julie also had to cooperate constructively. These sessions were extremely painful and confronting, and the whole period was confusing. Julie and I lived apart for a few weeks as part of the therapy, and I temporarily moved in with my parents. Mothers are strange creatures, let's face it. My mother not only embraced me in her heart but also literally in her arms in a chokehold from which I feared I would never escape. Somehow, I found the necessary inner peace, and the storm subsided. Just as suddenly as the waves had struck, they ebbed away, and our crisis seemed to be over.

"Let me take a look, son. always those problems." I stood in the bathroom with my upper body exposed, arm raised, and my mother inspecting my armpit up close. It seemed like just yesterday that Mom was drying me off in the same bathroom as a 5-year-old boy with those rough, air-dried towels. My trip down memory lane was painfully interrupted by my mother's index finger pressing on a swelling in my armpit. "Damn it, Mom, that hurts. What is that?"

"There seem to be a few pimples popping up, I'm afraid. Are you allergic to anything?" I leaned over the sink to inspect my armpit up close. Three emerging pimples arrogantly stared back at me without any hint of embarrassment. Painful.

"Shit, Mom, I don't see any other option but to sew those chamois into my shirts. until I've properly analyzed the problem and know what the real cause is." By evening, I returned home relieved, my car loaded with ironed shirts equipped with chamois. Now, without the outside world knowing, I could continue to drip and pour until the root cause was resolved.

And now here I sat, facing this interested duo 3 days after Julie had found the solution. Julie woke me up as I turned into one large steaming dripping cave in my dreams that night.

"Harry, I might have found a solution. It is not an alternative to prevent your sweat stains but a treatment to stop sweating itself. It's done through Botox injections that temporarily block sweat glands, resulting in reduced sweat production."

What a woman! Julie explained that she had found this specific treatment on the website of a 'wellness clinic,' where women get new breasts and have their lips pumped. It didn't matter to me. As long as there was a way to tackle my perspiration woes, I was all for it! Julie promised to schedule an appointment for me, which was set for today. I left at 8 AM. It was 90 kilometers from home, and with the traffic, I expected a drive of over an hour. I informed Inge that I would be on location today with several potential clients. I asked her to pass on the message in case John or anyone else called me. The wellness complex was located about 10 kilometers from the coast on a hill with a beautiful sea view. The sun was hesitantly peeking through the clouds. It promised to be a fantastic day, and if I left here, back home, my sweat problem would be squashed.

At the reception, I was greeted by a fresh young girl, about 20 years old, who clearly enjoyed life.

"Good morning, sir, welcome to the Wellness Center. How may I assist you on this beautiful day?" It was only because she was exceptionally beautiful, with curves that were beautifully accentuated by her tight white apron cinched tightly at the waist with a white belt. Because I was in such a good mood with the promise of sweat-free armpits otherwise, this artificial welcome would have been enough for me to turn around. She verified my appointment in a schedule and then handed me a large green towel and a white bathrobe wrapped in transparent plastic to indicate that they were washed and hygienic.

"Before you start your program, an intake interview will be conducted with you so that we can better tailor our approach to you," Sonja, as I deduced from the name tag pinned to her right breast, said to me with a smile.

"You'll go through that door on your left, then at the end of the hallway, there's access to the men's changing room where you can store your clothes and belongings in a locker. You put on your loincloth, wear your bathrobe, don't forget the locker and towel key, and then walk through the salon doors to the cabin behind the changing room. You'll have your intake and receive the program for the rest of the day there." I must say, Sonja's explanation was very clear, and the way she delivered it, structured and in short sentences, made me very relaxed. Did she also give massages? Body to body?

"Well, Mr. Jones, have a good day and enjoy your stay with us." She had handed me a white pouch with a string at both ends as the last item. I looked for the opening of the bag to put my clothes in.

"Sorry. Um, Sonja, but this bag is broken. It won't be possible to put the clothes in there." I handed her the bag.

"No, Mr. Jones, that's not a bag. That's the loincloth I just told you about. You put it on after you're completely naked and have stored all your clothes in the locker." The way she pronounced 'naked' was simultaneously neutral and exciting, but probably unintentionally.

Loin cloth?

I walked through the designated door into a dimly lit hallway while Indian choirs softly sang to me, and spicy scents reached my nostrils through smoking incense sticks. Behind the door, at the end of the hallway, was the men's changing room. There was no one there. I stripped off my clothes, stored everything in the locker, closed the door, and hung the cloth in front of my genitals while tying the strings on my back. The whole concept eluded me completely. This couldn't have anything to do with hygiene, as there was complete freedom under the cloth. Everything hung and dangled in absolute freedom. The intake room was white with several mirrors on the wall, a metal stool, and two modern black leather club armchairs opposite each other. The metal felt cold and hard against my buttocks. I had placed my legs slightly apart so that the loin cloth hung between them like a white flag, indicating that I had surrendered.

Olga sat in the chair to my left, Nameless to the right.

The term 'Wellness center' had misled me, and now I was here in an asylum being bombarded by two doctors, probably colleagues of my own, Julie, asking all sorts of difficult questions about my perspiration problem.

"You understand, we need to know all that to assess the actual cause and, therefore, what impact we can expect from the treatment," she said, staring at me with her green almond-shaped eyes hidden behind dark-rimmed glasses. I thought of 'One Flew Over the Cuckoo's Nest,' of which I remembered many white coats but no loincloths.

I answered the questions fired at me, which were carefully noted down. Suddenly, Olga stood up, approached me, and asked me to lift my arm.

"That doesn't look too good, Mr. Jones." She pressed on one of the bumps my mother had also drawn attention to. With little desire to go through the whole armpit saga again, I nodded in agreement.

"OK, we know enough. You'll receive the program from us. Enjoy it!"

A light reassurance came over me. I had a program in my hands, given to me by Olga. The intervention on my armpit was scheduled for 3:00 PM. Before that, however, I had the following on the agenda:

- 10:00 to 11:00 AM: full-body massage
- 11:00 AM to 12:00 PM: thermal baths and Hammam
- 12:00 to 1:00 PM: light lunch

- 1:00 to 2:00 PM: sauna

- 2:00 to 3:00 PM: relaxation and preparation for intervention

- 3:00 to 4:00 PM: Hyperhidrosis armpit treatment

After that, it was over, and I could go home.

A full-body massage to start with.

Olga led me to the massage cabin. A small room, dimly lit, with a massage bed in the middle. Moody exotic music played in the background, and a soft scent of aromatic oils filled the room. Olga told me where to hang my towel and bathrobe and that I could lie on the bed. The thought of my loincloth and what lay behind it caused slight panic. The term "full-body massage" can be interpreted in many ways, but I suspected that the massage could be stimulating enough and that there would be kneading close to the pubic area, with a heightened state of readiness. Somehow, I had expected a dark, exotic woman to come topless through the door and then lead me to the seventh heaven with her massage. So the surprise was great when Olga took the oil bottle and gently smeared and stroked my feet.

Through the mirrors in the ceiling, I saw the body of a man about 1.90 meters tall, slim and sinewy, not heavily muscled. His face was beardless and mustache-less. Gray-blue eyes, almost childlike, looked at me. Heavy eyebrows, a beautiful straight nose, a normal mouth with a full lower lip and thin upper lip, even cheekbones, and a slight dimple in the chin. Relatively much chest hair on the calmly breathing chest, not heavily developed biceps, at the sides of the belly slightly above the hips, the first signs of excess fat. A loincloth, with two hairy, slender, unspoiled legs protruding from underneath and large feet. The foot massage was delightful until Olga started pulling on my toes.

I counted along as she worked on them one by one. 1, 2, 3, 4. I looked at the ceiling to see if she secretly pulled one off and put it in her pocket. Olga wasn't like that. The view of her cleavage was particularly attractive. Would her breasts also have been the subject of a transplant, and how would such a transplant feel? Perhaps I should put on my brave shoes and ask her about the intimacy we were experiencing together. Her hands had by now worked up to above my right knee, where she was now playing with the muscles on the inside of my thigh with her long fingers. Someone threatened to awaken under the loincloth. It is often said that men can only think with their dick, which is the cause of uncontrolled bacchanals. With that, my current action could be considered revolutionary because, with my full mind, I concentrated on my friend, as it were, to get into the cockpit and undermine the erection. And it worked!

"Are you OK, Mr. Jones?" Olga asked as if she had noticed the tremendous effort I had just made. The left leg was now up. Every time Olga moved, she ensured her fingers or hand remained in contact with my body. A trance crossed me, and I abruptly sank into a deep sleep without dreams, images, and tension. Nothing. Just sleep.

"Mr. Jones, Mr. Jones. the massage is over. Please stay calm for a moment longer. Then you can get your bathrobe and towel and go through that door to the baths and Hammam."

For a few minutes, I lay recovering. The hour had flown by, and I wanted to stay here for a day, floating in a universe without consciousness, enjoying nothing.

In the space of the thermal baths, I discerned a few female figures through the steam. Apart from the fool who interrogated me during the intake or the guy on the massage table, I hadn't seen any other men. Well, there weren't many men getting breast enlargements.

Slowly, my feet felt their way across the light blue mosaic at the bottom of the pool. The water was warm and smelled of sulfur. In two corners of the pool, showerheads were attached about a meter above the rim, from where streams of water gushed forcefully into the bath. Under one of the showers stood a woman, around 40, I guessed, with her head slightly tilted forward so that the jets had free reign on her shoulders and neck. I should try that, too. I waded through the water toward the corner of the bath, a figure swam past me, water splashing in my face as I approached the shower. The force of the jets was so strong that I struggled to stay upright. Like lashes, the water streams struck between my shoulder blades and my neck. Under the pounding of the blows, my two body halves would soon be separated from each other, thereby solving the problem of the left armpit for my right side and vice versa. I stood there, trying to convince myself that this was healthy and pushing aside the thought that I'd have the same effect after a good wrestling match. In the middle of the bath, I took another shower, which seemed to mimic the effect of a calm waterfall. I swam over and positioned myself underneath. Spontaneously, my eyes closed to enjoy the water curtain falling over me fully. An ultimate moment of absolute absence of the here and now. My head was perfectly centered under the water veil, my eyes closed, and all my facial muscles completely relaxed. A feeling of perfect happiness in pure emptiness of mind and thought.

The woman who had let herself be hammered under the other shower emerged from the streams towards me. She positioned herself about 30 centimeters away from me under the waterfall. She, too, spontaneously closed her eyes. For a moment, I wondered if my loincloth had anything to do with it. I was lying on the water's surface before me and held back from sailing off to other places within the pool by the strings around my waist. However, my float was securely anchored, so I decided that the lady, like me, was experiencing a moment of supreme bliss. The woman was slightly smaller than me but certainly tall for a woman. She had mahogany-colored hair tied back in a ponytail. A few gray streaks peeked through the dyed hair, and it had something charming about it. Her scalp was shiny and tight, her lips full and round, but her neck remarkably wrinkled. Round, brown, stiff nipples scanned the water for pirates on the coast. Rarely had I seen such large, beautiful, natural breasts. The anchor was lifted. Automatically, I reached for the loincloth, pulled it down, and tucked it between the legs, which I clenched tightly together. It seemed like time to go to the Hammam.

The "Do you come here often?" caught me off guard because somewhere, I had expected that speaking wasn't allowed in these baths, just like a smoking ban in public spaces. As it turned out, it was a rhetorical question, and she knew it herself. Beth came here weekly for her hour of relaxation but also had at least one procedure per year. She had made quite a few friends and now went on vacation to a Club Med with three other ladies she had met here every year. Did I know how old she was? Again, a rhetorical question, but the answer would be less innocent.

"38?" I ventured, taking into account my own age and the potential nature of the procedures she referred to. Her smile was like that of a child being told how well she could count for her age.

"Almost. 51, dear!" That was truly unbelievable; maybe it was worth considering undergoing some of the same treatments as Beth before my 50th birthday. Unsolicited, she listed the restoration works that had been carried out. An eyebrow lift, a forehead lift, a full facelift, a Mesolift specifically for wrinkles, two eyelid corrections, injections in the lips, buttock liposuction, breast augmentations, and a vagina rejuvenation. I stood there with my mouth agape, staring at the extraterrestrial being. She looked remarkably like a human female. Any moment now, her eyes would turn yellow with snake-like pupils, and green slime would ooze from her mouth or rejuvenate her vagina like lava flowing into the water.

A vagina rejuvenation? A vagina rejuvenation!

"You've gone all out with all those renovations," I blurted out. Beth took my comment seriously.

"If you take the step, you have to do it properly. It's all or nothing. Today, they're going to perform a neck lift."

She stared ahead, swallowing. I heard the sound of water moving a few meters away from me, where a figure glided through the basin.

"Once, I was so beautiful. I used to stand in front of the mirror in the morning and be impressed with myself. I never got used to it; every time was a surprise. Men worshipped me, and I had so much power," Her lips trembled, eyes closed.

"What happened?" was on the tip of my tongue, but thankfully, it stayed inside because something told me I didn't want to know. What I did want was to feel her breasts, not from an erotic perspective - too much mystery had been removed for that - but out of pure curiosity. I had undoubtedly seen many fake breasts without knowing it, but to my knowledge, I had never consciously felt one. And the pair lying next to me in the showcase seemed exceptional, so I had to feel them. Beth's face tensed. My idea of starting a conversation about her breasts was disrupted by the attention the Designer Vagina received without asking.

"I have four children from four different men. They're beautiful and have all the best qualities of me and their fathers; they're four little angels. But my vagina suffered trauma from the tissues, resulting in decreased voluntary control and muscle tension, which has its impact on sexual pleasure."

This was told neutrally, giving me the impression that Beth was talking about a patient rather than herself. The trauma had not been limited to the genital tissues.

"Uhm, and are you satisfied with the procedure?" I blurted out. The question thankfully evaporated before reaching her.

"The problem is that you still have to have a sex life, of course," she laughed bitterly. "I don't understand why men aren't interested anymore. First, you have everything, and suddenly, nothing. Do you understand that? Can you tell me what's so unattractive about me?"

"Honestly, I don't know you, but I find you an attractive woman as far as I can see." She smiled, revealing her pearly white teeth. Luckily, she didn't interpret my remark as an invitation to reveal the rejuvenated vagina from under the loincloth.

"Your breasts are of unparalleled beauty," I said to keep a clear focus.

"The doctor has devoted a whole photo report to them, which is on their website as the reference for breast augmentations," she said proudly. "You know, there are different techniques for performing breast transplants, through the nipple, injections through the muscles, and through the navel, of which mine is an example."

"How. how does it feel to have fake breasts?"

Suddenly, she grabbed my right hand and closed it around her breast. I had a perfectly round bosom in the palm of my hand with a rock-hard nipple between my index finger and thumb.

"Wow!"

I stood in front of her and grabbed both breasts. Our loincloths drifted over each other. It was a bizarre situation that didn't arouse any excitement in me. Still, it did satisfy my need to feel the difference between pure nature and artificial. Honestly, I didn't feel a clear difference, only that perfection had been matched here. It was time to go; the light lunch awaited. I let go of her bosom and made to leave.

"Thank you," she whispered. The tears on her cheeks mingled with the shower streams.

I had a light lunch in a room with beach chairs and a buffet. Four ladies were poking at their plates with forks. Everyone was lost in thought, which suited me perfectly. While I consumed mussels, salmon, and gray shrimp and washed them down with a glass of Chardonnay, I tried to distance myself from stretched skins, breasts pumped through navels, and rejuvenated vaginas.

After the meal, I sank into a deep sleep.

"Mr. Jones, Mr. Jones."

I opened my eyes and looked into Olga's face.

"It looks like you needed your sleep. It's quarter to three; we need to hurry. Follow me."

Although awake, I remained in a daze for the rest of the afternoon. The procedure on my armpits, the so-called Botox injections, which were done under local anesthesia, escaped my full attention. A sweat test was performed, indeed concluding that I suffered from hyperhidrosis. In addition, orange dye dots were applied to the shaved armpits, making the most active sweat glands visible. It was quite a colorful scene. Finally, the marked skin area was injected with multiple Botox shots.

With the anesthesia still in my arms and the impact of the massage and thermal baths still in my system, I drove back home irresponsibly. Fortunately, I had an automatic car because changing gears would have been a disaster. Steering was already quite difficult, causing me to take twice as long to complete the whole journey. Arriving home, I stripped off all my clothes, stared at my painful armpits in the mirror, and then sank into bed, drifting into a deep sleep.

THE TRAP

Bumper to bumper. "Seven kilometers of traffic jam," the voice had told me after the 8:30 AM news. Today, it was not because of the routine queuing of the car stream that was pushed through the funnel every morning but because of a severe pile-up in the morning fog. Three trucks, two passenger cars, a van, two dead, four seriously injured, two of them critically, thousands of vehicles in a row involuntarily blocked by accident, thousands of cars on the other side yearning for a glimpse of wreckage and blood-stained dismembered limbs. I saw stress, frustration, and anger around me. Appointments went awry, speed demons felt short-changed, drivers were not quick enough to the accident scene, and others expressed their chronic dissatisfaction. I thought it was all fine. Until recently, I was one of them too. I usually rush at 8 o'clock to get to the car on time. Laptop between the back seat and the front seat. Blazer from my suit on the hook of the left back door. Cruesli bars in the right pocket. Phone in the car kit.

After my nightly worrying and analysis of the cause of the wet, clammy misery under my armpits, my mind became much calmer for a few days now. In concrete terms, however, nothing had changed in the symptom because the bodily fluids continued to flow despite the Botox procedure. The misery had become even worse: for starters, I had lost €300 on that joke, the impact was minimal in my opinion, the growing stubble under my armpits caused terrible itching and irritation, and I dreamed of enormous evil breasts that hissed me on the heels were already shouting "We will get you" And my left armpit had also woken up Julie suggested that we should file a complaint with the Wellness clinic or take up my story with some consumer interest group. For the time being, I let it pass as my perspiration continued to flow.

So I wore my shirts with chamois. I don't think there is an immediate gap in the market. But for me, they worked well during the period of pouring sweat. Of course, I kept thinking about the exact cause. Couldn't the problem lie partly in the private sphere? With a third party in 'the making' and Julie's volatile distrust, I thought I had every reason to do so. Yet I was inclined to believe that the real core was related to my professional use of time because I was experiencing intense happiness with "My" family while the professional worries and concerns of Value Creators Inc. seemed to distance themselves from me. Ben and Sam were two excellent lads. Julie was a top child psychiatrist and a top woman who, miraculously, still stuck with me. The main indication was my armpits, which showed no dampness at home.

And the distance that I mentally felt growing silently towards Value Creators Inc., I experienced as a relief. I realized that I was also starting to create that distance physically.

More and more often, I found myself wrapped in a chamois-stitched shirt, locked in my car, driving from one fictitious appointment to another, enjoying the crystal clear tones of Daniel Lanois' Shine (or Talk Talk's Spirit of Eden, or Simple Minds New Gold Dream, or Texas' Red Book,) that came to me through the 12 Bang & Olufsen speakers in surround sound. The sound from my stereo was of such a class that I had checked in the rear window mirror several times to see if Mark Hollis and his associates from Talk Talk were not in the backseat playing an intimate acoustic set. That turned out not to be true. Talk Talk had already split years ago. I had always enjoyed driving, and the daily moment of closing the car door, starting the engine, and hearing the album of choice resounding was always a little bit of paradise on earth. I wandered around that pleasure resort every day until I drove into the driveway of our house. In the past, at times of heavy stress, I sometimes wanted to take a detour to enjoy myself a little longer in my cocoon and to take the necessary distance from things before entering my private life. At the time of my escapades, I was lost in another paradise of carnal pleasure and 'misused' my car to get home as quickly as possible, cheering myself on the way because of that damn meeting that had run over another 2 hours and that kept me from getting there to enjoy my Julie and the children.

Now, however, I had entered a phase where my car journeys from home to the office and back became car journeys that eventually allowed me to listen to entire playlists and eventually degenerated into "Home to home travel.". At first, I still took care of tactical contact with my secretary or even John so that I could continue to drive with a comfortable feeling and enjoy myself in a relaxed manner. With my iPhone connection installed, the possibilities were endless. I was toying with the idea of setting a new world record by listening to all the songs on my iPhone while driving. Potentially, that would involve 7,500 songs for an average of 4 minutes, allowing me to drive for 500 hours. The only permitted stops were to fill up with petrol and sanitary breaks. It seemed like a challenge and a wonderful experience. In anticipation of that significant world record attempt, I happily toured around, usually in the BMW X5, sometimes in the Volvo Bertone. Isolated from everything and everyone in my own universe, just a spectator of what was happening in the outside world, without being a participant. Here, I felt at ease, confident, and not afraid of my own imagination or the thoughts of others. Untouchable, peaceful, like an embryo in the womb.

I remember a newspaper article about a man who, every morning for 17 years at 8 AM, got on his bike in a dark gray suit, ironed shirt, perfectly knotted tie, and lunch box under the tie-down strap on his way to university where he was a Doctor Emeritus in chemistry. However, in 17 years, he never arrived at university. After all, he always cycled to his mother's, where he spent the day behind the curtains, reading a newspaper, playing cards with his mother, at 10 AM sopping the sandwiches in the coffee that mother was so good at making, eating soup at 12:30 AM, watching TV in the afternoon, explaining the soaps to Mom until the brass clappers of the solid oak clock struck 5 PM. Then Mom would get a kiss on both cheeks, and he would leave with a "See you tomorrow" into the evening. It took no less than 17 years before his wife discovered that her husband had been unemployed all that time.

Or that successful surgeon who, for no less than 25 years, made his entire family, friends, and hospital with which he was associated believe that one promotion after another was a fact and that money was earned and could be spent like water. 25 years! Then the banks had enough, and it turned out that the boat, Saab convertible, and houses in Switzerland and Spain had been financed by a CV of which not a single letter was genuine. Every day, he went to the medical university to hone his theoretical knowledge further.

These kinds of human dramas have always interested me because they are funny, scary, and relatable at the same time. And so terribly painful. The all-consuming fear of not being able to meet expectations leads to unprecedented creativity, and the most fantastic lies in some and to a life of paralysis or suicide in others. And although not at the same "Niveau de tristesse," I had also descended into a kind of professional vegetarion during this period. I could no longer pursue new customers, monitor project teams, think strategically about the organization, or be a guest speaker at conferences. I stopped taking myself seriously. Or rather, the only person I took seriously was myself because only I seemed to understand that life is a farce where we are groomed to take ourselves seriously, grow up and be a successful adult, and pursue goals that are based on somehow related to 'what you have achieved' in terms of prestige. And I was pretty much into that farce myself. I went along with it by completing an excellent university education "Cum laude," then landing a traineeship at McClaud & Cloud, networking like crazy, and finally joining Value Creators Inc. to be brought in as the young dog bursting with ambition and potential. It seems like yesterday that I started there. The drama of this wonderful journey was that I had become attached to all the material comforts that come with such a steep career: my house, my business class travel, my Church shoes, my Ralph Lauren polos, my Scapa suits, My car! That was still small compared to John's or Will's capital, and I may not have had that perspective at all, but I had certainly fallen into the one-way street of "Always more." I was in a trap that had hitherto blocked every thought. I had nipped in the bud a possible alternative, a life outside Value Creators.

This year alone, I was tempted to make the following purchases: an iPhone 15 pro that I used to work, jog, and ride my exercise bike. What an invention. Let's think the Walkman in the eighties and the portable CD player in the nineties were innovative.

I purchased that exercise bike about 5 months ago after I saw my belly's size increase in the morning mirror (nowadays, I could happily fit the tip of my right index finger in my navel!). Peter, in his office, 'had seen toiling on such a steel horse. He was very pleased with it and recommended the Finnish Tunturi for €2500. Peter took his cycling sessions very seriously. Every day he was at the office, he climbed onto the saddle between 12 and 1 PM, dressed in a bright yellow suit that fit around his body like a condom. He wore very special bright red pointed shoes; they looked more like slippers and a fluorescent shiny teardrop helmet with matching low air resistance sunglasses that looked somewhat like a windshield. He didn't care what others thought of his hobby and outfit, and it slowly became a familiar sight on the 6th floor. I had even heard it said that he now received clients for a meeting while sitting on his steel steed, and Inge typed out the contents of presentations while he puffed and quoted. Without all other accessories, I would have purchased the same bike, which has since resulted in at least three sweat sessions of 45 minutes per week. Although I had no idea what the impact was on my weight, as I never stood on scales, it was certain that my condition had improved, and I also felt sharper psychologically. Unfortunately, the idea that all the sweat spent cycling would limit production during the rest of the day turned out to be untrue. The music on my iPhone actually kept me going through those boring sessions. During the first week, I empathized with a cyclist who, clearly without doping and under his own power, climbed one col after another. The very first time, by the way, it must be said, in all honesty, the second climb was so exhausting that I had to dismount at a heart rate of 185 to continue on foot. Those first times, I cycled in line with the philosophy that the Dalai Lama adheres to, namely focusing 100% on the one activity you are doing at a certain moment. An activity that you have to give yourself completely to, whether it is drinking tea or working hard on an exercise bike. In this way, you are the most pure and enriching for yourself and your environment. Now, I couldn't really imagine that the Dalai Lama had ever ridden an exercise bike in his orange robe because, despite the lack of a real chain in which the textiles could easily get tangled, it would still be an extremely awkward affair to even not to mention the temperatures under that robe. I usually sat very lightly dressed on my machine and not in full uniform like Peter. Still, the heat I experienced, which turned into copious amounts of sweat, was unprecedented. After a few rides on my exercise bike, I was sure that Dalai's philosophy made no sense. I hoped the good man would never be tempted to mount an exercise bike because he might have some shocking insights.

The imaginary Mont Ventoux was killing me after a week, so I simply let the playlists do their work. It is crucial to be on the pedals to the tune of the correct "Playlist." When I took one hairpin bend after another to Cult music, I burned at least 200 more calories than if I let Pink Floyd or Nick Drake lead me up the hill.

In addition to these relatively small gadgets, I had expressed a possible anticipation of the midlife crisis by spending €17000 on a second-hand Volvo 262C Bertone. A silver-gray Volvo coupe that is no less than 45 years old. I remember the Volvo Bertone from the era when my father bought a new Volvo every 2 years, and my brother and I went to the local Volvo dealer with Dad on Saturday mornings to pick out the new model and the new color. Now, a new model was very limited in Volvo's terms as the '200' models hardly changed in appearance for 15 to 20 years: they remained clumsy cars with enormous bumpers that oozed the notion of safety. However, in 1977, Volvo, including my brother and me, amazed the car world. A special coupe was born through a unique combination of Swedish (boring) solidity and Italian design. Built based on the 240/260 models, a lowered 2-door coupe was constructed with all the luxury, such as walnut inlays, soft leather upholstery, and air conditioning. A total of

7,000 262 Bertones were built from 1977 to 1981. The world press reacted very differently. Some talked about the ugliest two-door ever made, and others talked about one of the most stylish coupes ever created on the drawing board. The fact is that the largest sales market besides the United States was the Eastern Bloc, where the leaders of East Germany, in particular, provided large orders for the extended 262 Bertone, which perhaps implied that Volvo was considered the Lada of the Western world. It's a matter of taste not to argue. Years later, the collaboration between Volvo and Bertone resulted in the 780, which the Italian actually co-signed, but the appearance was less successful in my eyes. My father had to limit himself to the 240 models, and my ownership of the 262 was limited to a glossy brochure that I cherished between my small, greasy hands or under my pillow during nightly dreams, transformed into the first coupe driven by children.

Early this year, I woke up on a Sunday with a strong urge to track down a Bertone on the Internet that day. I 'googled' frantically for a 262C Bertone, which gave me dozens of hits. It turned out there was even a Bertone club. Several Bertones were offered for sale within European borders at prices ranging from €3000 to €20000. However, I found the most beautiful example in California, where the first owner still decorated it in the summer. It was a steel blue metallic copy that had only driven 100,000 kilometers, offered for the price of $ 17,000, which made a significant difference in Euros. The car was in fantastic rust-free condition, which the Californian sun had certainly played a role in. The interior was also passable, with hardly any traces of use on the seats, which is an exception because typically, the leather is damaged in a dry, sunny climate and leads to cracks in the leather. In short, that car had to become mine. Payment could be made via Paypal, which I mainly used to finance my Bootleg CDs ordered via eBay. Danny Blaker owned the car. After some emailing, we contacted each other by phone. Blaker was a retired Volvo car dealer who spoke passionately about the Amazon, 480, and 262 Bertone. The guy had developed problems with his blood vessels due to excessive cigarette consumption, which had caused not only problems with walking but nowadays also with driving. The good man had to say goodbye to his great love in a wheelchair. It's bizarre how you feel an immediate bond with people you've never met and come into contact with purely by chance, as if you've known each other for years. Danny was such a figure. We kept in regular contact, and Danny arranged everything for the transport so I could pick up the car on March 2 at the port where it had arrived in a container. I hadn't slept the night before, like an excited child waiting for weeks for the holiday that finally starts the next day. Julie found it entertaining and touching at the same time. When I saw the car for the first time, I was overcome with emotions because of the release, the beauty, and the nostalgia. Before I started the engine and drove home, I caressed the leather, the wooden dashboard, and the inlays in the doors for at least half an hour.

We were still standing still. Actually, I had a very mixed feeling, which I found difficult to acknowledge, namely, on the one hand, the status I had achieved, the prestige and all the material things I was sensitive to and, on the other hand, the absolute emptiness and boredom in what I did and a complete lack of belief in the added value that I and Value Creators Inc. delivered. I had become a huge snob who, in the process of growing up, had forgotten to shed his humility. The snob was stuck in his troubles and in a traffic jam. Ambulances and fire trucks had passed. I felt like I was still standing in the same place even though we were now 45 minutes closer to death. My GPS indicated that I could leave the road in 7 kilometers. That would take a while, but I would take that exit for a change.

"John" indicated my display as the phone rang "Psycho Killer" by the Talking Heads. I answered it reflexively.

"Jones, where are you? I've been waiting for you for half an hour." I tried to concentrate. Appointment, appointment What was it today? Tuesday.

"Jones!" John shouted impatiently. Tuesday. Oh hell yeah, we had an internal meeting to work out the options for Spensers' deal.

"I know, John, but I'm stuck in a traffic jam here. You should listen to the radio, or perhaps better yet, turn on the television. Things are tough here Several deaths. I have no idea how long that will take, but I have a meeting at Goldsmith at 11 AM. First appointment with the HR director, who had read those articles in eHR Mag and contacted us." Not everything was a lie; I was part of an immobile string of cars.

"You could have fucking called me," John fumed, seeming to have bought the rest of my story.

"Sorry, John, I had to iron out some wrinkles at home." I wasn't really creative, but apparently, I was credible. I decided not to answer any more phones, turned up the volume, and continued dreaming.

The turn I had taken led me through small idyllic villages whose names came from the Middle Ages. Nothing here pointed to a relationship with the modern city. It was now a quarter to ten, and I wondered what my plan was for today. It was a beautiful spring day, which, now that the mist had lifted, was characterized by a clear blue cloudless sky and a temperature of 15 degrees, as the display on my dashboard showed. Driving around aimlessly with the sole objective of 'Driving around Aimlessly.' Less pointless than it sounded. Julie had appointments today in the morning, but I think she was free in the afternoon, so maybe we could do something fun together and then pick up the kids early.

With enthusiasm, surprised by my own spontaneous inspiration, I left a message on her answering machine. Enjoying the views, a graceful watercolor depicting a lovely hilly landscape of various fields, bushes, and cow pastures, and Keane's 'Hopes & Fears,' I continued my ride. Suddenly, David Byrne showed up again. That had to be Julie. I answered without looking at the number.

"Harry?" That was clearly not Julie, but I always recognized that voice out of thousands. Marc, damn it, Marc. We hadn't spoken in forever, but this was one of those rare friendships in which the frequency of communication or reunion was no indication of closeness. In my opinion, unconditional love only exists on two levels: one between male friends and two between grandparents and grandchildren. Women among themselves, with all due respect that is nothing but misery. I saw that at Value Creators Inc., where several girls had become extremely close, and at times, it was impossible to separate them. Jennifer and Inge were a wonderful example. My secretary for years and one-time body painting model, Ed's other secretary. Jennifer came in through Inge because the two had been best friends since their training as management secretaries. They were always together during lunch breaks and at company parties, where they danced intimately and provocatively with each other. And suddenly, it was over; God knows why, at least I still haven't, but from one day to the next, it was hatred and envy. The experience of this was non-verbal and verbal; it looked like two fishwives, and also physical. Insofar as I had ever doubted the stereotypical scratching and hair-pulling of two quarreling female beings, that uncertainty was decisively dispelled by the two leading actresses themselves, whom I found fighting and screaming in my office one late afternoon 6 months ago. Although the door was closed, I had already heard some commotion in the hallway, which did not lead me to suspect that World War III had just broken out. Since the ladies had barricaded themselves on my desk and in my leather chair, respectively, while clothes, hair, and organs were being pulled, I believed, driven by my male ego, that the ladies had thrown themselves at each other because of me. "Hey, hey, hey, Inge, Jennifer, ladies, let's discuss this like adults now," I soothed. "Jennifer, I thought it would never happen to me again, but if you really insist, I would like to paint a view on those breasts of yours. I didn't know it was known and so high, so I propose." Unexpectedly, I also received a blow from Jennifer, after which the ladies, supported by their own verbal incitements such as "Bitch", "Whore" and "Slut", once again attacked each other. Pieces of clothing flew around. Jennifer showed off a firm breast wrapped in a tiny lilac lace bra. To avoid spontaneously broaching the subject of body painting again, I turned around and left my office. I also noticed with Julie that friendship among women was not as transparent, deep, and sincere as pretended. There were no physical wrestling matches or vulgar insults organized. Still, for reasons inexplicable to me, intensely close relationships suddenly ceased to exist, or labels such as 'a top chick' were unceremoniously exchanged for 'saw a woman.'

The easy thing with men is that your best friend has always been a dick, and both parties know it and share that opinion. Marc was one of those, a dick to rely on. In my student days, he was, next to Fred, my source of support when it came to drowning in our tuition fees, exam success or disgrace, heartbreak, and spending nights building up our philosophy of life. And, of course, Marc was also my music mate, the man I went to concerts with, still by the way, and organized listening sessions to critically analyze the new LP by U2, REM, or another obscure group while enjoying a bottle of Pastiche or Whiskey to subdue. Nowadays, we see each other a maximum of twice a year, at least once in a family context, so as friends among each other, our privacy is very limited. And yet, when we emailed or saw each other, we were always immediately on the same wavelength. During the time that Julie and I were apart, followed by our therapy, Marc was always there to support me. Also, it is to make fun of me and tell the truth. That was not about taking sides but about believing in someone unconditionally. I also noticed the same bond between my parents and Ben and Sam. The expectations that parents, implicitly or explicitly, to a greater or lesser extent, project onto their children work like a gigantic burden and hinder unconditional love. How many children become estranged from their parents sooner or later or experience that love is mortgaged by unfulfilled expectations? Grandparents are free from those expectations that make absolute, unlimited love possible.

"Marc, my man!" I shouted enthusiastically. "Tell me, when are we going to crack one again?"

"I'm already cracked." It sounded ironic and stuffy at the same time. I don't have a sixth sense, but in situations like this, my brain activity goes into overdrive in an ultimate attempt to anticipate what is to come in the hope that it will make reality less difficult. Out of fear that this is the most dramatic thing imaginable, the worst diseases and scenarios come to mind. Terminal cancer, child accident, being fired, divorce,

"Do you have a moment?" my buddy asked.

"Yes, certainly, always for you," I tried frantically.

Marc and Joan were also our best friends as a couple, and the children got along well. Marc and Joan had already given birth to three, and despite the many warnings given by my friend, my sperm had ignored all the advice from Victor, Stan, and Lis. Victor was 6 months older than Ben, Stan was only a few weeks older than Sam, and Lis had just turned one. We had already been on holiday together a few times. However, our agendas did not allow us to go out together again this year. Joan had been Marc's one and only crush after a series of fleeting adventures. Joan was different, mature, full of humor, sharp-witted, mysterious, and had a classy appearance. She may not have been the prettiest girl in class, but she was certainly the most attractive. Long black hair curly over the shoulders, a full round face with dark brown eyes, a light upturned nose, and full lips. Approximately 1.70 meters tall and of normal build. At university, they were a couple from the third year onwards, and since then, they have been inseparable, madly in love, and intensely happy. Marc and I have been living as Siamese twins since our first day at the age of 13 when we bumped into each other at the bus stop. There were usually three of us, or even four of us with Fred. I thought Joan was fantastic.

Marc and Joan were a model couple for Julie and me. Marc completely missed all the vicissitudes, escapades, and therapies. "Why do you have to make it all so complex?" was his standard response. Well, why I would have liked more of my friend's peace and stability because although he fits the 'house, tree, animal' picture, his life seemed vibrant and enjoyable. Even when the children came along, everything apparently remained under control and easy, and none of the stress I experienced with Ben and Sam was noticeable.

Since Lis was born, Marc had sometimes jokingly said that three kids disrupted the balance, but I don't think he was serious about that. Lis was the apple of his eye. What was the secret of their lasting love?

"Eeeuh, Harry, I'm dealing with a few setbacks at the moment." Now it's coming, I thought.

"Shit, mate, not too serious, I hope. Tell."

I lowered Kate Bush's voice to a whisper and maneuvered my car along a narrow asphalt road.

"God, I don't really know where to start. On Monday, I had to be checked for pain in my kneecap. You know, I've been thinking about that for a while. Well, Damn, I have cancer in my right leg, there's a malignant growth under the kneecap. God knows where it came from." I decided not to respond. Marc wasn't ready yet.

"So my right leg has to be removed; there is no other option. In two weeks, I can register for the Olympic Games for the disabled."

I went off the road and, after frantic attempts to keep control of the steering, came to a stop in a ditch. I opened the door, climbed out of the car, completely hanging with its right side in the ditch, and gasped for breath.

"Then something else happened, which is actually my biggest concern at the moment. Stan was hit by a tractor in front of his school yesterday. It all happened so quickly. I stood there; that tractor wasn't going fasthe farmer hadn't It was like in slow motion. He is in a coma in the hospital where I am now heading because the bright spot is that he responded this morning. Joan was there all night, and I took care of Lis and Victor. The doctors fear for his brain. He suffered a skull fracture, and the question is whether the damage can ever be repaired." I heard Marc swallow on the other side. The sun's rays were warm and burning on my face; a buzzard circled high in the blue sky, climbing higher and higher via an imaginary spiral. I thought of Talk Talk's 'Colour of Spring' and the first song, 'Happiness is Easy.'

"Based on the first scans they have done, although not absolutely certain yet because they won't get the right picture until he wakes up, we have been told that we should expect delayed mental development or even mental growth that is not happening goes beyond the development of a 3-year-old child."

I didn't have time to recover and take everything calmly, so why should I? It was his story, his misery. It wasn't about me. I walked a bit around my car, which was stuck deep in the ditch up to the wheel axles. Help was needed.

"These will be exciting days. Wish me luck. Another not-too-pleasant event has occurred It all sounds a bit surreal, but you just have to think like this: there are also people who win the lotto.. Anyway, Joan is a lesbian. I caught her a week ago."

Jesus. Today's mobile phones can take a beating and are apparently 'waterproof.' I noticed this when I fished the device out of the ditch and placed it back against my ear.

"Marc, Marc, are you still there? Sorry, I don't want to tell you all again, but I missed a part you literally cut out, if you know what I mean, so you have to let me retell Joan's story. What I heard about it probably isn't right either."

Whether it was because of the moisture in my cell phone or the wind blowing past me, his laugh echoed hauntingly. It was one of those moments where your emotions are confused, and there is no proper synchronization with the way they are expressed. When I was five, and my father came to tell me that my grandfather had died, I felt deep sadness and started laughing out loud.

I still didn't fully understand what I heard. I saw Marc without a leg, Stan with his eyes closed, connected to all kinds of tubes and IVs in a hospital bed, and Joan with another woman. It was difficult for me not to burst out laughing. After all, this was such a disaster scenario, which only suited British gloomy humor, which Marc and I could normally appreciate. But if it happened to yourself, you were not expected to find that funny, let alone laugh at it.

"Joan, you know, my Joan, the woman I have been happily married to for more than 15 years." That lady is a lesbian. The advantage of today's multimedia world is that you can also catch your wife virtually, and it is not necessarily physically necessary to be between the sheets." In a flash, I saw Julie making love to Joan in our bedroom. Hmmmmmmmmm.

"Have you ever heard of dating lines? Those lines you call to arrange quickies with other sad soulmates. You know. Fuck I probably don't have to explain it all to you; you'll know damn well what I'm talking about. You'll have to give me the number you're calling soon. Let's see if a single father without a leg is still popular with certain kinky chicks." Frankly, Marc overestimated my expertise in this area. I had never called a sex or partner hotline before, but it didn't seem like the right time to do so now.

"There is also a line where women meet with each other. I had huge telephone bills for a few months, and although I made a lot of calls abroad, I still thought the amounts were a bit too significant. So, I checked my account and saw a lengthy list of 099 numbers. That didn't mean anything to me, so I called there. I didn't know what the hell I was hearing. A sultry female voice informed me that I was connected to the largest network of women of all shapes and sizes but willing for women. As a "Horny goat," as the male caller was addressed, you were connected incorrectly and were redirected to another hot number. Harry, I thought it was a joke, an error by the telecom company in which calls made by others were conveniently sent to us, and we were distracted. That was my strongest belief, and if Joan hadn't reacted out of fear that she would one day be caught, ironically, she could have gotten out of it without any problem. But she burst into tears when I told her that evening I had discovered a huge error on our invoice. I was floored by her explanation; where once aware of the reality that conversations with other anonymous women aroused my Joan, I initially saw possibilities to enrich our sex life and an increased chance that my fantasy with two women would be realized. But it's not all that innocent. That erotic line turns out to be just part of a sex life that takes place between Joan and other women. She has a friend, a female manager at work, and she has been simulating her orgasms with me for over a year. Harry, I can tell you that will give your male ego a nice blow. Sometimes, I think I just didn't know; sometimes, it's so much better to live in a delusion than to have to face the truth. Anyway, it's over, she's leaving me. "The positive thing is that she wants to remain friends because she loves me and wants the best for the children." I thought I detected some cynicism in the last sentence.

"To complete my happiness, the icing on the cake, Harry, is I was fired this morning. There was already something in the air since those consultants were restructuring our business. I believe you call it a Business Process Reengineering, but I was surprised that it would go so quickly. Luckily, I was in the mood anyway, so that was possible."

Marc had worked for 13 years at the same international bank, working his way up to become an American investment fund expert. The bank had merged with another American bank 6 months ago.

"To sum it up, Harry. I lost my wife, leg, and job, and Stan probably lost his brain. To be honest, I envy Stan. If I had lost that, everything else would make little or no difference. But what more could you want on such a beautiful sunny day? It's a beautiful day; don't let it get away."

Now, slowly but surely, it all dawned on me. Didn't know what to say.

Marc had told his story in one long breath as if it were a great relief to be rid of it. That was, of course, impossible. I rather had the impression that saying all the events out loud was part of the consciousness process he was going through. I could even imagine him addressing himself in front of the mirror in the evening by repeating the same story a few times to make it completely clear that it was about him and no one else.

"God boy, they got you terribly. I don't really know where to start. God damn it, that leg. Stan and Joan, who would have thought. Eeeh, let's meet up quickly."

Our conversation was difficult because what can be said now? Marc had then told his story, and the space that now arose for dialogue was filled with bumbling in which one person was not waiting for a relevant response from the other, and the other had no idea what sensible thing to say. Men know and accept that from each other, expect nothing less, and prefer to dismiss uncomfortable topics with a joke. Marc and I usually interacted like this. However, today was different. The shit poured on my best friend was of such a nature and smelled so bad that no lighthearted comment could cover it. Speaking of a misplaced joke.

"Listen, Harry, I'm at the hospital. I'm going to Stan quickly. Think of me, and keep your fingers crossed for me. Call me and tell me when you are coming to look at my artificial leg."

"Good luck, buddy. I call you."

Absolute silence. Before me, I saw a watercolor depicting a green valley, a narrow stream meandering through the fields of corn, corn, and cleared land. The sun rose, or did it set? Hours had passed. I stared into the distance. Was I completely freaked out? Was I hallucinating? Was I delusional? These terrible images had come to me spontaneously, springing from my sick mind. I checked my cell phone, and through the foggy window, I saw Marc's number on the last call I received, at 11 o'clock.

The farmer had been extremely helpful; around 4 PM, I saw the red tractor coming my way in the distance. I had decided not to consciously attract attention, which I found a bit embarrassing. However, the good man himself had noticed me and had come to me to ask what had happened and whether I needed help. He had connected the back of my BMW to his tractor with cables. In a few seconds, my car was pulled free, and I had free use of it again. What a machine, that tractor, a Massey Ferguson. I thought about Stan, Ben and Sam.

It was 5:25 PM. Marc's phone kept ringing in my ears. I couldn't turn off the 'repeat' function. Cancer, accident, lesbian, dismissal. Cancer, accident, lesbian, dismissal. Four standalone words, with a mnemonic, KOLO or KOOL, easy to remember, had come together to ruin Marc's life. I drove into the garage exhausted, waited until

Depeche Mode's Enjoy The Silence died away in absolute silence at 6 minutes 48, got out, walked to the shiny washed Volvo Bertone, and ran my hand over the cold body via the mirror, door handle, along the petrol flap down to the trunk. God, how I loved that car.

OPTIONS

"Harry can give the status of Spensers in a moment, but now it's time for Diana to discuss the situation surrounding the government sector," said John, who led the management meeting. Every month, we sat together to discuss the state of affairs. "We" were John, the chairman, and our direct local boss; Diana, our star from abroad and responsible for the non-existent government sector; Ed, the coming man, the killing man, the career maker 'pur sang,' Melanie, in my eyes, a great entrepreneur, and myself, Harry Jones, 38 years old, dripping armpits and not entirely sure. Will only showed up sporadically. His responsibilities extended far beyond the local region, which involved a lot of travel, and if he was present, it meant a crisis in the tent or a moment of ego trip because, under his ultimate responsibility, a wonderful contract had been won elsewhere, which he also did with wanted to share. As always, we started at 9 AM. The agenda consisted of looking at the entire business from our annual plan and discussing any staffing and human resources issues. So, each of us was allowed to comment on the numbers projected on the screen that were related to our accounts. A distinction was made between the revenues, the projects sold and invoiced, and the expected sales of future projects or the pipeline. I wasn't completely there today, or actually even less than usual.

Writer

World traveler

Keymaker

Chambre d'Hote – B&B

Drummer

Hunter

'Hunter' had been my latest addition to the list of possible alternatives for my professional career. I had been carrying the list with me for a while. Since the intervention on my armpits, and especially the realization that it had done nothing, I still spent the day in my chamois shirts; I had started to think about possible alternatives for my future outside Value Creators Inc. It was now clear to me that my current professional context unconsciously made me so unhappy that the moisture was desperately seeking a way out through all my pores, specifically my armpits. In fact, the idea of writing a book had occurred to me as a response to the completely absurd story told by my friend, Marc. You didn't make something like that up, and it could lead to a crazy scenario in book form. Since it would, at the same time, be extremely morbid schadenfreude, I abandoned that theme for the time being. But the idea of becoming a writer as an alternative to my career seemed like something to me; there was something romantic, soloistic, and rebellious about it. I had never written a story before, except, of course, speeches, presentations, and reports where so much nonsense was normally sold in a credible manner that I initially saw myself writing fictional nonsense. Imaginatively, I could already see myself doing that, withdrawn alone, the bottle of red wine within reach in the dimness of a musty attic room lit only by a few candles. Children were sleeping peacefully, and Julie was lying wonderfully naked under the sheets, waiting for my arrival, musing about her great romantic who had written a beautiful bestseller. So, for now, I left this avenue open and put "Writer" at the top of my list.

Diana was standing next to the flipchart and had just drawn two ascending lines from left to right across the sheet. The red line represented the income, I learned for the umpteenth time, and the black line represented sales. How long had she been with us now, coming over from London? At least a year, or maybe two. Yes, it was already before Ed's promotion to Director. Nothing has sold yet, and two beautiful lines have repeatedly appeared on the flipchart. Now, an amount also appeared on the board, which was then circled with a blue marker.

"We now know for sure that the Potential Market Value is 95 million Euro per year and that our competitors are bringing in 50 to 60 of that, so the good news is that, conservatively estimated, we can sell 25 to 30 million per year."

It was communicated in a manner that made it seem as if the contracts had already been signed and the first invoices could be sent out. John was euphoric.

"Diana, that's fantastic work. We can be sure that this will become a significant part of our local business in the future. Good job."

What had I missed? In my experience, the only difference from previous times was the figure "95 million" with a blue line drawn around it. To be honest, I had never understood Diana's added value since her arrival, although I had also heard the stories about Dirty Diana. I decided not to ask any further questions. Ed wanted to add something.

"This seems to me to be a great example of a good analysis that makes it clear what our potential is and allows us to make the right investments without unnecessary business development." Once again, the relevance of the comment escaped me. I couldn't stand that guy anyway for all the evil he embodied. My mobile phone notified me of an incoming text message.

'There used to be two, but now there is only one,' I read on my display. Marc. The day of the operation was apparently over and successful. It depends on how you look at it. After the dramatic phone call when I returned home, I spoke at length with Julie about the tragedy that had struck my friend.

She found the story of Stan's cancer and accident horrible.

"Joan lesbian Ha, I always thought so. I think she even had a crush on me." I choked on my wine. Women. I thought it was a bold statement. "I thought you were friends," I responded.

"Yes, why.? I'm just saying that I always suspected Joan saw more in women. Remember when I turned 35, and we organized that party? I never told you, but when we said goodbye when you were standing outside with Marc looking at his new car, she suddenly twisted my tongue." It sounded quite triumphant to my ears.

"But you don't mean that. You never told me anything about that. I thought we had no secrets from each other?"

Fortunately, the painful silence was short-lived. Beef that you are! Julie apparently decided not to pay me back in kind. The logical "Why don't we keep secrets?" was omitted.

"What difference would it have made? I thought she was tipsy, and even though something told me she likes women, I didn't want to fuel your imagination."

We then talked about the impact it would have on the children, in which Stan's situation would, of course, also be decisive. Julie clearly dismissed the loss of his job in this violence of bidding (very, worse, worst) as the least serious. "You lose a job, so what? He will probably get paid a big bonus because they can't just throw him out after 13 years." We classified Stan's accident and possibly permanent injuries as 'number one.' Marc had called me at the beginning of this week with the happy news that Stan, who had been out of his coma for more than 10 days, would apparently only be left with a speech impediment from the whole affair. He had suffered a very specific injury that affected the muscles that control his mouth and tongue. "He will have to practice a lot, and even then. but that's OK, after all the bad predictions." He also informed me of the date of his amputation. The situation with Joan and his dismissal were not discussed. The priorities were clear. So now the leg was off. "Be careful with what you have. I'll call you later," I texted him back.

God, doesn't every person want to be a world traveler? It makes sense that it will be on a list of possible alternatives. In the distant past, namely the responsibility-free student, Julie and I had traveled for 3 months on a "No budget" basis in Cambodia, Vietnam, India, and Thailand. We had collected money for the various flights, but other than that, we had nothing. Real adventurers, we had been confronted with the most exotic insects and vermin as sleeping companions and new dimensions of "Un-hygiene." Looking back on it from a nostalgic perspective, something like that is always fun. It must be said that my idea of the world traveler, as I had it on my list, was not one who traveled through the world accompanied by Lonely Planet and Rough Guide with long, unwashed hair. Mine traveled and stayed first class, using trendy guidebooks such as the "Cool Hotels & Restaurants series and 'Five Stars on the Globe.' However, that world traveler met two conditions that were missing from me. You had to have one and not the other. Money and family obligations. In short, not exactly a feasible story, but based on the belief that "You have to keep dreaming," I left this option on my list and started playing the lotto fanatically.

"Harry. Harry!" All eyes were on me.

"Was it so sleep-inducing?" Diana asked grumpily.

"No.. uh no, I was just walking through the last projection for Spensers."

"Great," said John, "you can share all that directly with the group. Diana, thanks again for the update. Harry, the floor is yours."

I dare not pretend that my explanations, made up off the cuff, are legendary, but this one certainly was, and unfortunately not because it was so smooth, clear, structured, and convincing. I rambled on about the real issue Spensers was facing, the size of the opportunity, our strategy, and the timing. In short, I voluntarily slowly crawled up, tumbling over the branches, to the core of the pyre. 2 Lines, a red and a blue, or a green and a black for a change, so simple, I couldn't draw them on a flipchart. After 20 minutes, Spenser's vessel was empty, which cannot be said for my perspiration source, which showed increased activity. I felt the absorption capacity of the chamois shirts being exceeded. It was certainly not the first time that a proposal from my side was received this way. No, it was actually that way as standard, just like the entire course of the management meeting, but where I was interactive in the past and knew how I had to parry these kinds of discussions, I now fell silent. I didn't feel like being defensive, either. So that meant swallowing.

"Harry, it must be just me, but I don't see any common threads nor any clear progress from a month ago." I didn't have to respond, and others did that for me. Ed first.

"I don't know, Harry, but if I listen carefully to you, the situation can perhaps be summarized as follows." I dropped out. I didn't care whether it made sense; I wasn't prepared to listen to a summary of this bladder. I bent over my paper, giving the impression that I was listening intently and taking notes furiously.

The possible option of a key maker came to mind when I remembered my visit to the key maker for a spare key for the Volvo Bertone. I had only just gotten the car and had one set of keys, which didn't reassure me, so I went to the key maker on a Saturday morning. The precision and dedication with which the man bent over his machine made a perfect duplicate of my key intrigued me very much. A nun entered as I waited on a stool, listening to the hum of the machines and their whistle. She wore an off-white floor-length dress with a gray pointed hood and a black cross on a chain visible on her chest. Hidden in the hood was a young, handsome face. She turned her hat back. Reddish hair in a bun was visible, along with an open face, dark brown eyes, and narrow lips. I estimated her to be between 25 and 30 years old. Her natural beauty radiated from her. The activities that were supposed to lead to a new key for my car were temporarily stopped.

"How can I help you?"

She showed an old-fashioned brown rusty key of excessive size.

"This key is from the attic room of the abbey, but here it has been broken off. Look, here is that piece. Can it be repaired?"

The man examined the key minutely, and I did the same with the nun.

"When I'm done with this gentleman, I'll help you. Please take a seat."

The machines started turning back. A new key was born. The nun looked shyly in my direction. I smiled, after which she resolutely looked away. The key for the attic room of the abbey. That interested me, a key that gave me access to a completely different world. To be honest, if the nun next to me had been a grizzled 80-year-old mother superior, my thoughts would not have deviated from my key and my Bertone. Now, however, under the shy, watchful eye of the young nun, I saw different scenarios pass in review, and slowly, my imagination started to run wild. An attic room where the ladies played ping pong and football in their robes on Saturdays then became a dark, dimly lit room where people drank and laughed and where the sisters had to confess daring stories to each other one by one, and then a room of easy morals where habits were changed was raised and whips cracked.

While I was paying, I heard the key maker suggest that I deliver the key later in the afternoon so that she wouldn't have to wait and he could immediately see whether everything was functioning properly. The nun thought it was a wonderful idea. In my mind, I saw the newspaper headline 'key maker left to live in excessive bacchanal'. As a key maker, you experienced something again; you gained insights into worlds that remained closed to others. My current list certainly did not include an overview of practically feasible careers. That selection had to be done at a later stage, but the series as it lay before me was the result of an initial brainstorming session, from which the key maker emerged as one of the favorites.

"And why don't we offer three weeks of free investment to work out the business case with them? If it makes sense, they should either continue or pay us. I think." I heard Diana say. Apparently, Ed's turn was over. He was staring at me with satisfaction.

'Chambre d'Hôte (France or Italy)' was the next option on paper. Perhaps that was the oldest idea for an alternative outside of Value Creators Inc. Actually, that was even separate from my current problems since Julie, and I had been talking for as long as we knew each other about this idyllic dream that we would fulfill 'Once we had the means. We had never specified that further, so this had always remained an 'ongoing' project.

"Agreed," Harry? Is that a correct analysis? In that case, "I see a future in it." John looked at me. I was expected to respond. I decided to live up to expectations; sometimes, it's that easy and better for everyone.

"That seems to me to be absolutely correct. We say the same thing, so I can certainly agree with that." That was enough. John looked away, Melanie started talking, and I went back to my notes. Everyone was satisfied.

Drummer. God, that seemed like a fantastic thing to be a drummer. I am not a drummer in some local brass band or unknown show band, but a drummer in a world-famous rock band. Think of Steward Copeland from the Police, what a drummer he was!, Phil Collins from Genesis, James Mclachlan from The Hunters, Larry Mullen from U2, Manu Katche, who had performed a lot with Peter Gabriel, and of course Keith Moon from The Who. All heroes were cool guys who were the backbone of their respective bands. I had also discovered the sticks in high school and was bitten by the bug for 4 years. From the age of 15 to 18, the only thing that existed in my universe was a drum kit.

All my adolescent frustrations were channeled into drum solos. Under my mother's leadership, a neighborhood action group had been set up to get Harry Jones off the sticks. Although all kinds of deep arguments were used ('But don't you see that you are wasting your future.'), it was clear to me that it was only a sound issue. I happily banged away in my attic room, with the window wide open if possible. I wanted to be fucking heard, and my talent had to get air. My father didn't understand the fuss, perhaps because he usually didn't get home before midnight, and by then, I was literally out of control in bed. So, Dad also saw financing soundproofing as a wasted investment. While the action group grew in size and was considering appropriate steps, a few friends and I started the school band The 'Master(de) Baters,' which could never become a band of world fame because of the name alone. Marc provided the vocals, Fred played electric guitar, and Tim played bass.

We were very impressed by this band name, which we believed would be perceived as intelligent and clever. In reality, it was a product of our adolescent minds, and no one got the joke.

We went on tour. A dream came true. On Wednesday afternoon, we drove in the van from our school's music room to the local club, a youth center next to the church. We had gotten Kurt to join us and lug around our materials, his worn white T-shirt bearing the gaudy handwritten word 'CREW.'

The action group 'Silent Nights' finally achieved success. Contacts had been made via contacts with the youth center The Future' actually, it was not surprising that The Master(de)baters was a bridge too far. To see whether a rehearsal room was available for all this violence. Apparently, it took some convincing, but under pressure from local residents, we were admitted. The rehearsal room was a small stage at the back of the cave that had been converted into a bar, where weekly parties for teenagers from the village were organized.

Many first kisses were received or shared here, as well as fist bumps and blows.

I wasn't much of a clubgoer. And now, suddenly, we were allowed to practice there on Wednesday afternoons, which, given the setting, actually meant that we were performing there. At least, that's how we saw it. We made posters on which we announced in a big way that 'The Master(de)baters' would move into 'The Future' as we always called the club, as part of their tour every Wednesday from 3:00 PM to 4:30 PM. The lost souls who came to play a game of table football on Wednesday afternoon, timidly drank their first pint, or played the pinball machine were clearly unaware of the piece of pop history that was being written in their presence. The Master(de)baters the only band that plays in The Future.

However, my drumming career ended abruptly when 'The Future' and therefore mine too, was reduced to ashes on a Wednesday evening. Arson. The perpetrator was never caught, and therefore, we will never know whether there was any connection between the classic 'Burning Down,' which we played for the first and last time that afternoon, and the sad end of the youth club. We had composed the song earlier that day and were so excited about it that we recorded it on tape while playing it five times in a row. Fred still has that tape, and it has become a tradition for us to listen to it together during my annual visit to Barcelona. I think 'Burning Down' gets better with every listen, especially because of the tight drumming that reveals more and more secrets. I have always admired drummers, and I smelled an opportunity when drawing up my options list. My age may have been playing tricks on me, but still.

"But have they ever considered at least outsourcing their payroll?"

Spenser's case still dominated the discussion. There was a lot of chatting, apparently without intervention on my part.

Hunter. It's not obvious (what is?) but intriguing. Ever since the morning walks with my father through wet dew fields, mossy forest paths, and autumnal carpets of leaves, nature had an enormous attraction for me. On holiday during the autumn holidays, we also went out to experience the hunts for big game such as wild boar, roe deer, and deer during the game season. Although far removed from the actual battlefield, at the age of eight, in my brown corduroy pants, dark green winter coat, and camouflage boots, I felt like a whole man and a full-fledged hunter. There was something magical about the hunting, the men moving like shadows through the dawn and mist, the excited dog barking, the rustling of brush and breaking branches, the blast of hunting horns, the short, loud bangs. A piece of it was shot to pieces at one point when a sea of buckshot riddled a young fawn before my eyes. The credibility of the myth that hunters maintained or helped the natural balance by only shooting old and sick animals was debunked and had an almost as traumatic impact on me as the forced knowledge that Sinterklaas did not exist. The image of the 'Good Hunter' who saved animals from their misery and helped nature, that romantic image, had always stayed with me, and I wanted to pursue it as a hunter.

At Value Creators, in addition to golfing, there was also a lot of hunting, in the literal sense of the word. Will, John, Ed, and Diana were avid hunters. This observation led to a hunt organized by John on one of his domains last year. Our large, wealthy boss had an 80-hectare hunting estate, which turned out to be a small area among hunters, but where we as a management team could let ourselves go unabashedly. So, the annual management team event was postponed from early summer to fall. Since I was a teenager, I had last experienced a drive hunt. I myself had never used a rifle, except for some childish shooting with an air rifle. Naturally, I became one of the hunters, and there turned out to be fewer hunters than the number of hunters, but that didn't spoil the fun. Around eight o'clock in the morning, there was a gathering at the entrance of the domain. In the large parking lot, it looked like a comparison test of SUVs and Jeeps. Volkswagen Touareg, BMW X5, Mercedes ML, Porsche Cayenne, Range Rover. It was all there. Will used a branch to draw the route in the sand that we would drift down and explained each person's role. He would open and close the hunt with a trumpet, two short strokes for the start and five long strokes for the end. The floats had to operate in a row and make a lot of noise, always maintaining eye contact with each other and ensuring they remained visible. The floats consisted of about five people: Alex, Youri, Frank, Melanie, and myself. Hilde was still recovering from her miscarriage, or at least didn't feel like confronting Ed, for reasons that were understandable to me. The hunting group consisted of Will, John, Ed, Diana, who looked like Zorro with her green cape and black hat, Harry, our retired partner who was still there for these kinds of occasions, Peter, Rob, and Patrick. The hunting group made a detour to a large open field that lay on a slope and ended in a coniferous forest. Our task was to drive as much game as possible straight into the sights of our hunting colleagues. About 20 meters was the distance we tried to respect between the floats. Apparently, I had not put on the best clothes because, after half an hour, I was trudging through the bushes, chilled and soaked with sopping shoes. We had already heard some shots in the distance, the shooting at the expense of some partridges and pheasants. Frank walked to my right, Melanie to my left. At times, I didn't see them, but suddenly, they appeared again. Communication was only with thumbs up and nodding. We ignored the brambles, spruce branches, nettles, and everything else, which resulted in the necessary welts and abrasions. A wild boar suddenly darted out from under a bush about two meters in front of me and started running, almost causing me cardiac arrest. Finally, after an hour and a half, we arrived at the forest's edge that led to the meadow where the hunters were stationed. Shots had been heard for some time as the game ran far ahead and ended up in the shooting field of our colleagues. Consternation everywhere. Shots fired from all sides, dogs barking, howling of hit game, Frank's screams. He was lying just a few feet from me. Folded forward in the wet, long grass, a shoulder blade shattered, and hail spread across the back. Fortunately, the man turned out to be out of danger, which apparently required much more or much less blood, but an ambulance was certainly required. The shooting of Frank brought a drastic end to the hunting party. Will didn't have to blow five long strokes through his trumpet. The shots my colleague had taken had come from Ed's rifle, which had also taken most of the game. The police arrived after Ed had been taken away, not entirely by the book, in my opinion, but since it was clear that this was an accident, the interrogation was limited to some administrative formalities, such as checking Ed's permit. In addition to Frank, seven pheasants, three partridges, four hares, eight rabbits, four deer, and five wild boars were shot that day. Not bad loot. Frank did not return to Value Creators Inc. Besides Hilde, Ed had eliminated his only other direct competitor. We had this year's 'Will Event' in a few weeks, which was less spectacular as it involved an ordinary barbecue at the man's home. Despite all the grim experiences, the profession of hunter seemed to me to be a beautiful profession, one with nature, alone but not lonely. I would aim only to go for the old, weakened, and sick games. I saw myself becoming some kind of hero of the animal kingdom, who, by the way, had also taken care of most of the game.

It could turn out to be a meager list upon further filtering, but for the moment, I was satisfied with it, especially because of the enormous variety. I folded it carefully and put it neatly away in my wallet.

"OK, so I'll summarize. We invite Eric Spensers to visit our HR outsourcing center in Budapest as soon as possible. Harry, you wrote it down? Your 'To do'.

Value Creators Inc. itself was, of course, still a possibility. Ultimately, there was no sign (yet) that the company had any problems with me. My armpits had serious problems, and in my opinion, this was a direct derivative of an underlying dissatisfaction with my professional context. Maybe only temporarily. In any case, it would not be wise to dig my own grave or end up in a negative 'self-fulfilling prophecy.' And the money was easily earned. I probably had to and could get rid of the hatred I had for my colleagues.

I nodded, gathered my things, and left the meeting room.

THE BARBECUE

"Should I call the police?"

"Call the police, are you fucking crazy. If you want me to lose my driver's license AND car for the rest of my life, then I would definitely do that. .Eh."

My head was spinning: at any moment, it could come loose from the hull, and the vomit would be peanuts compared to the mess that would then occur.

"You. you don't have to do anything. Don't worry I'll just wait until tomorrow and." There was no point in resisting the new blast of bile, debris, and goop that was coming through my stomach, esophagus, and trachea, making their way to my mouth and nostrils

"Harry? Harry.is everything OK?" Julie's voice now sounded deeply concerned.

"Tell me where you are. I'll put the boys in the car in their pajamas, and I'll come get you."

I hated to think of Ben and Sam seeing their father in such a state.

"Mom, .mom, daddy coughing!" both shouted in unison as I tried in various ways to forcefully say goodbye to a hangover that had taken possession of me the night before. Value Creator's Inc. had gone big with its New Year drink, and the sparkling wine had made way for champagne Heidsieck & co. Pouring myself full of champagne until I drop is not necessarily the image I want people to associate with Harry Jones, but the attempt I made that evening was not a half-hearted one. It's amazing how easily you can walk in the freezing cold, with a temperature of -10°C and frozen snow on the sidewalks, in your shirt and without shoes (to be honest. I realized after 10 minutes that my shoes were no longer participated, but did not find it an insurmountable problem.) covered a distance of 9 kilometers within 2 hours. It is perhaps even more surprising, or at least disturbing that such an exercise is apparently not sufficient to sober up, and I have to conclude that the quantities of champagne were such that the sobering mechanism could not operate long enough to prevent me from waking up around 5:30 AM mid-sprint from our bedroom to the bathroom. And even though my head, with my mouth hanging open, was about a meter and a half ahead of my feet, I still arrived too late. One learns by doing; the third time I was well on time, I was able to sit quietly on my knees and patiently wait for the moment of the upward thrust with my elbows on the edge of the toilet and my head in my hands. And then suddenly, Ben and Sam were behind me. I was happy that in my sons' eyes, Dad only had trouble coughing.

I was convinced that I would not get away so easily now. How many times had I said I thought I was dying.? Poser. Now, it was different. There was no stopping it. Perhaps the spinning of my head was a phase in the transition from earthly life to the afterlife. Damn, could that even exist?

I looked around. My dashboard, my windshield, my steering wheel. Everything was covered, and the stench was unbearable. Goddammit, I was on my way to hell.

"Harry?!"

"Julie. Really, go to sleep. Everything will be fine. When I come to my senses tomorrow, I will drive home quietly. I'm sorry." Before a discussion could develop about the sincerity and meaning of my expression of regret, I disconnected the call.

I just managed to flatten my chair and sank.

Our babysitter, Virginie, 17, had canceled at the last minute.

"Just go alone. Ultimately, I don't know that many people, so you don't have to hold back. Promise me you won't drink too much because it's quite far."

"And so I have an excuse not to make it too late."

However, Julie looked fantastic today and I regretted not being able to introduce her to my colleagues. They would all be jealous.

It was a bright evening during the last weekend of May, and Will couldn't have had a better time at a barbecue. Will was John's boss and a guy in his mid-40s who had made it. Like it or not, Will had 'arrived'. Will had proven intelligent and slick enough to become International Director for the entire European & Middle East Region in 12 years. I could still learn something from that despite my 'fast track.' I had actually only dealt with Will in the management meetings, and sporadically, I had the honor of being able to give him some explanations. Then he was to the point and a bit short: 'Upstairs in 5 minutes.' 'Now!' when he called me. 'No' or 'Not now' were those sporadic moments when I had to contact him. Will had invited his entire management team following a mega deal of 50 million Euros over a period of 3 years. I'm telling you, Will had it made.

But I didn't know that Will lived in a castle and owned 2 Jaguars and 2 Porsches. I did something wrong. I parked my BMW at a safe distance, carefully examined the building from the outside, and then walked into the garden in the direction indicated by arrows. 'Park' was a better description.

Everyone was there, including supporters.

"Hi, Harry. Where is that beautiful wife of yours?"

John was there too and always modest. As he shook my hand and patted my shoulder with the other, the smell of alcohol hit me in the face.

I didn't have to bother explaining Julie's absence because John had performed his own showpiece, Elisabeth. We shook hands as John introduced us. The situation was a bit awkward, as it was at least the 5th time we were introduced to each other in honor of some occasion. Elisabeth's smile was always the same, but there was no recognizability on her part. The feeling of discomfort was probably just for me. Her hand slipped from mine; she turned and disappeared among the other guests, directed by John, who held her by the elbow.

"Look who we have here."

Will stood in front of me pontificating. At his side was a somewhat shy, not unpretty woman of about 45 who looked worn and tired, with a body that was on the border of anorexia. Before she was introduced to me as his wife, Harriette, Will definitely ruined my evening: "I hear from John that we are making good progress at Spensers, with an expected first contract within one month at the latest. Harry, that would be very good because it would allow us to skyrocket in sales and turnover, and since we have some setbacks elsewhere, that is right on time. Well done, Harry! Value Creators Inc. is proud of you! That deal of yours is going to be our Trojan Horse at

Spensers. That is an absolute cash cow for the coming years. We'll drink to it later."

Harriette's downcast eyes suddenly opened at the sound of her name. "This is my wife and rock, Harriette. It is important that you have a strong woman behind you who understands what you do and why you do it. That is the key to success in a world where 1 in 3 couples divorce! We have been married for 12.5 years this fall, and we are going to celebrate that big time, honey." Harriette's hollow eyes, which continued to stare at me, made more of an impression than Will's blah blah.

"Harriette, this is Harry, a real hotshot from our country. Product from our own home, grown and shaped within the ponds of Value Creators, soon to be the celebrated man again because of a 15 million deal. I remember I had some doubts during the recruitment interview when John presented me with your candidacy, but I made the right decision, you can see."

Besides the fact that I had no memory of a job interview with Will (at the same time, I was impressed that he knew my name!) I wondered who his words were intended for. It was clear to me that Harriette was not immediately excited by the description of this unique person to whom she had just been introduced, and it did not interest me either. Will also thought it was enough, nodded at me, put an arm around Harriette's narrow shoulders, and disappeared. Harriette hadn't spoken to me.

I craved a glass. These kinds of occasions were not for me. When I was able to go there with Julie, I usually behaved like a little child hanging on to Mom's skirts all evening. It wasn't that I couldn't communicate or animate, but it simply didn't interest me in a Value

Creators setting and made me feel extremely uncomfortable. On the other hand, Julie managed to integrate with great ease and found the meaningless lightheartedness spread by egocentric people who considered themselves extremely important particularly amusing. I was on my own tonight, which didn't bode well in my current state of mind.

In addition, I was clearly not very motivated in recent weeks. My conscious search for the professional options in my life had a distance. A process of increasing indifference towards Value Creators Inc. set in motion, which meant that tonight's party could be stolen from me. I had mainly spent the past week driving around in my car, with hardly any contact with company colleagues. The few times a colleague called me, I felt disturbed by my busy activities, such as compiling my favorite Top 5 (which 5 albums would I like to have with me on that clichéd desert island), and I reacted irritated. It could all be stolen from me.

On the way to Will, I went through the Top 5 again to make sure that the choice was now final. I was relieved to conclude that my absolute Top 5 (with a ban on one and the same band being found multiple times.) were the following:

U2: Achtung Baby

Talk Talk: Spirit of Eden

Sisters of Mercy: Floodland

The Hunters: Sounds of Emptiness

Lloyd Cole and the Commotions: Rattlesnakes

Will's champagne, Cuvé Privilege Will Johnson, tasted excellent to me. I shook hands and walked through the crowd, eagerly looking for that one colleague who would make me feel comfortable. I strolled from one group to the other, received friendly pats on the back, and endured the standard jokes and the bluff about 'that huge mega deal'. But I didn't connect. To prevent my 'shammy shirt armpits' from being unable to absorb my sweat for the first time and me dropping out prematurely, the champagne did its job more than adequately.

An hour later, I found myself at a long table, still quite actively part of the conversation at first. The mood was there. I was surrounded by colleagues with whom I had spent about 65 hours a week for years and with whom I now, of my own free will, was chatting and dining on a summer Saturday evening. Diagonally to my left were Youri and Alex. Youri was in his mid-40s, single, completely bald, over 2 meters tall, and very slim, making him look taller. A smart bird but so terribly boring. There are amazing but true people who really don't know an ounce of humor and just don't know what it is. The humor chromosomes haven't come through. I had already wondered several times whether Youri was of German descent, but when I asked him that during a company reception after there had been an embarrassing silence after a sharp joke from me, it turned out that he had analyzed the entire family tree the following weekend and I was informed, first thing Monday morning, that nothing was happening, and why I wanted to know that anyway.

Youri is incredibly professional, 'reliable and solid' as it would be defined in the evaluations, and Melanie knows that all too well. She uses him as her slave, and the slave knows that obeying means 'Eating' and resisting means 'Caning.' In that sense, Melanie is fair: Youri has not missed a single promotion yet. Alex was a different case. A very hard worker and, to be honest, a really good consultant, very analytical and strong in communication. What bothered me about Alex was his political views, or rather racist beliefs, that he displayed at every opportunity. I had never had a conversation with him without talking about all kinds of exotic immigrants. Alex's entire array of aliens was impressive. Turks, Italians, Moroccans, Indians, Pakistanis, you name it. Alex had seen me looking in his direction, and my eyes were focused on the white wine bottle. I smiled at Alex once, gestured to the bottle, hoping he would serve me, and shouted something in his direction. "Hey Alex, everything under control?" Satisfied with the statement, he filled my glass and started a conversation with me while gesticulating. The meaning completely escaped me since he was sitting on the other side of the table. I caught parts of sentences. After a few minutes, I understood that the several times spoken or understood me, "Cow. mee. sow.." had to be interpreted as "Romanian gypsies" who would bring our civilized world to the abyss to lead. I didn't feel like dealing with this nonsense any further because I knew that Alex was not too creative in coming up with nationality-specific problems or cultural differences. My gaze moved past the various guests to Melanie, who was sitting directly opposite me, between John and Wilbert, her husband. Wilbert was one of those modern men who had put aside all career plans to give his wife the space that emancipated women deserve. Wilbert took care of their only child, took her to school, did the housework, cooked, picked up the daughter from school at 4 PM, did her homework, washed her, and waited for Melanie to arrive. A beautiful division of roles that commands respect but did not increase my respect for either Melanie or Wilbert. On the contrary. I thought Wilbert was anything but a guy, actually, a wimp if I let my male ego give his opinion. Not that it really bothered me, but when I thought about it for a moment, like tonight when I saw Wilbert beaming next to Melanie, I couldn't imagine any intimate carnal relations between the couple. Of course, that didn't say anything about reality because maybe he was oversized. Wilbert was always in a good mood whenever I met him and always up for a good joke (perhaps a characteristic of well-hung men.). Wilbert sat next to Diana tonight, to whom he apparently made a smart comment because she seemed genuinely interested in what he had to say and couldn't suppress a burst of laughter. Wilbert is next to Diana. That was an interesting setting. Diana Dirty Diana Came to our office via a transfer from the London office 2 years ago as Director to set up a local Public Sector branch. She could stamp, Diana. It was said that she had been transferred through her husband. This top British official secured one of the largest contracts in the history of Value Creators Inc. and had taken care of it by signing it. I had never met the top official, but I assumed that the pale, middle-aged guy next to Diana, who was sipping his red wine and staring into space, was her 'Husband.' When his slender hands lit a Benson & Hedges and then reached for the stiff upper lip, I knew for sure.

Diana had been the 'bid manager' on that contract, and after the deal was closed, she was immediately catapulted to become the new hotshot within our organization. That's how it works at Value Creators Inc. It was never really clear to me whether they already had a relationship at the time of the contract, but in any case, Mister Diana's power was strong enough to also force a transfer for his lovely wife when he was transferred. The top official remained silent, although Wilbert also regularly talked in his direction. I felt a little sorry for Mr. Diana, especially because I strongly suspected that here and now, tonight, he became aware of the full impact that contract had had on his subsequent life until today.

After her arrival at the office, Diana soon had a reputation for being a man-eater. I didn't understand any of that. To me, she was a blonde vixen without any charm: hard, blunt, cool, and she also walked like a farmer. I always thought of Pam Shriver, the tennis star from the 1970s and early 1980s who moved like a duck over the sacred grass with a size 10 wide legs and feet turned outwards at a 45° angle. Strangely enough, Pam Shriver still had something feminine about her that I couldn't say about Diana. With Pam, I always wanted to know what was under the skirt. I definitely didn't have that with Navratilova (who, by the way, usually wore pants over a pair of phenomenal cycling calves.) or Diana.

Anyway, if it were true about Diana and all those male colleagues, You might also start walking with your legs apart and feel uncomfortable. According to the corridor echoes, Will was a constant factor among all the comings and goings at 'Diana station.' In addition to being a company waitress, Diana was also our very own Lady Di: she had made it a point to imitate the real Lady Di when it came to hairstyles, black clothes, and eyes. But despite all these fantastic assets, our Diana had not yet won a single contract, and the Public Sector meant nothing more to us locally than a lot of fanfare about 'identified potential market value,' 'pipeline,' and 'traction' during the monthly executive meetings. Every month, Will thought that things looked promising and that good progress had been made. I thought it would be a good idea to have the top official talk to Will, and maybe that would shed a slightly different light on Diana.

Diana brought in Melanie. It must be said that Melanie was actually the real hotshot. She had come from a competitor where she had had a meteoric career. She joined Value Creators Inc. as a Junior Director. At the age of 32, she was promoted to Director. Melanie took over corpses in her professional career, and that paid off, leaving victims behind. She was in the top 10 of 'Global best-performing Directors.' I wondered how many victims she had suffered in her professional triumph. I didn't know anyone who wanted to work with her, and most employees left the company after one intensive experience, except for Youri and myself. They are a bunch of losers, and I think Youri was a latent homosexual, so at least he had an excuse. For me, there was no clear reason. I generally enjoyed working with, and even for, women. Usually, I thought the women I worked with had a good sense of humor, except for Diana, whom I stayed far away from and with whom I had not yet had to do a professional assignment. Melanie was also quite an attractive woman, and of course, I preferred to work with that than with a scary ghost of whom you didn't always know whether you were talking to her front or back. Wilbert actually also had a bare-bottomed face, I thought, as he leaned towards Diana, showing his teeth and laughing.

The white wine was top-notch, a Puligny-Montrachet from Labouré-Roi from 1989. While Hilde talked to me and I took in the various table companions, I washed the powerful, light, dry, tongue-caressing white liquid through every corner. of my mouth. In combination with the foie gras that was now being consumed, this was a true paradise for my tongue and taste buds. Fortunately, he did not have to be distracted by the chatter of Hilde or other conversation partners.

"No, speaking to a customer in such a way is unacceptable."

I nodded in agreement to Hilde, who interpreted this confirmation as an invitation to launch a new interesting topic of conversation with impunity.

Ed sat next to the top official. Ed and Hilde. Ed was a wreck. It was unclear to me how this man could function. I have encountered many wrong, unethical people, but Ed and his ways beat everything. Ed is in his early 30s and married to Sonja, a young, attractive woman who radiates class and intelligence. Once again, she demonstrated this while she sat next to him. Ed and Sonja. What she saw in him and why she was still sitting next to him was one of my biggest mysteries after everything that had happened in the last 2 years. If they knew the story, reality soap producers would love it and would certainly be interested in the script.

Ed started as an ambitious brat at Value Creators Inc. 9 years ago, right out of college. From day 1, he explicitly stated that his ambition was the partnership at Value Creators. That's what he went for. As an analyst, he managed to impress the various Directors. His hard work and dedication were praised and resulted in well-deserved promotions and bonuses. Seven years ago, Ed revealed that he had started a relationship with Sonja, Will's secretary at the time. It was surprising news, especially because Sonja would normally have married her Marc that summer. Contrary to the tone within the rumor circuit, the relationship with Sonja turned out to be more than an affair, and more than a year later, Sonja and Ed had a grand wedding. It was striking how many heavyweights from Value Creators Inc. and customers were present at that party. There were fewer direct colleagues because they were not relevant to his anticipated career track. His peers did not like Ed. Based on several informal mentoring conversations that Directors and managers had with Ed's direct colleagues, a picture emerged of a driven career maker who was able to go above and beyond and had a pair of exceptionally well-developed elbows. However, as long as Ed couldn't be caught unethically, the projects kept coming in, and the customers were satisfied; no action was taken.

Sonja became pregnant almost immediately after their wedding day. Shortly after the pregnancy was announced, Sonja left Value Creators Inc. to work as an HR manager at a renowned local telecom operator. Rose was born. In the photos I can remember, and especially the one in the obituary, she looks exactly like her mother, with the same large dark eyes and intelligent look.

"Say, Harry, why isn't your wife here tonight?"

Hilde disturbed my thoughts. I took another sip of the wine as I prepared myself to say something meaningful to my neighbor. It was the least I could do to reward her for her perseverance. For the last half hour (or was it much longer?), she had been talking to me undisturbed and non-stop. I had caught certain fragments, but there was no way for me to follow through, and now I could simply pick up the pieces by answering an obvious question. Why wasn't Julie there tonight? In fact, Hilde deserved better. She was at Value Creators Inc. and started as a junior manager after being 'bought away' from a banking client. Peter was the Customer Director and had met her several times on steering groups where she had profiled herself so well that, at a certain point, we had made her a contract offer. That was 4 years ago. Hilde was small and a bit stocky, but I thought she had a feminine appearance and always knew how to present herself well. She had beautiful eyes that she knew how to draw attention to in the right way with subtle make-up, and of her body, she was clearly most satisfied with her breasts. Me, too. Small breasts, certainly proportionate to the rest of her physique, were displayed in a refined manner. Not vulgar, on the contrary, but prominent. Her sense of humor was great, as was her assertive way of leading conversations. I had done a few projects with her in the past where her negotiation skills and conflict management had really impressed me. The customers also walked away with her. Hilde and Ed had followed the same track for a long time, from junior manager to senior manager. They were always compared during the evaluations, with Hilde receiving a final ranking above Ed for the first time 2 years ago. I had hardly had any contact with her recently, and it bothered me that I was not able to have a real and sincere chat with her that night. But I was too much of an outsider, and the distance had increased with every glass of Puligny.

In the private sphere, no one really knew what her situation was, where she lived, whether she had a boyfriend, etc. Until more than a year ago, she was unexpectedly out of action for 2 months, of which two weeks she was hospitalized. Peter had come to the Senior Management meeting with the announcement, who was under no circumstances allowed to leave the four walls, that Hilde was pregnant and had been admitted for an abortion. Hilde pregnant?! It created some commotion in the meeting room that expressed general astonishment. Apparently, there was a perception on Hilde's part that being pregnant was not a natural part of her. And then we were also confronted with an abortion.

"Wow," Rob shouted, "She finally got a bite, and she let the fun between the sheets take away the result." Rob was always ready for a raunchy comment, which turned out to be appreciated by the majority because after an initial 'Oooh,' an atmosphere of laughter prevailed.

"Well, we actually just had a problem with the babysitter." He canceled at the last minute, so with two children, you know. Julie has been having more trouble with her stomach lately, stitches and such, so she could use some rest too. "The first months are always critical." I wanted to bite off my tongue when I saw the tears welling up in her eyes. What an incredible fool I was.

"Oooh, fuck Hilde, I'm sorry."

"That's OK. The confrontation is sometimes still a bit too big. Excuse me for a moment."

She pushed her chair back and left the table. My stomach turned. 'The confrontation was a bit too big,' yes, I understood that, but how could she be sitting here opposite Ed? Talk about confrontation.

Rob's comment had been the starting signal for a free grab in the grab bag of obscenity. Ed had joined the discussion: "There is such a thing as a sperm bank, so I wouldn't be so sure about that pleasure. Not that I don't want her to have it."

Ha, ha, ha, ha filled the room. Will also seemed to enjoy it all as, as chairman, he let the discussion take its course without returning to the formal agenda.

"Or maybe our Hilde still believes in gnomes." A bit like Sleeping Beauty, who lets herself be pampered by the seven dwarfs. I thought this distasteful display really went too far. This had to end. Like a true hero and moral knight who makes it explicitly clear to others where the boundaries are, I stood up, held my cell phone to my ear, and shouted just loud enough for everyone to hear: "Yes, yes, you have your say I'm in an important meeting, but take a moment to step outside. Just hold on."

A month later, I was working late one evening or had to close some transactions on eBay because the bidding period was almost over. And I didn't want to miss certain albums, especially if they were original bootlegs. I had checked into Diana's office, who was abroad for a week. Suddenly, I heard two voices in the office next to me. It turned out to be Peter and Ed who had returned from an important customer meeting for which Ed was the project manager and Peter the Customer Director, which meant that you could nod in agreement at important steering groups, posit best practices, make blunt comments, and all this under the guise of the experienced heavyweight being tried and tested through years of consultancy experience. It was surprising how little you had to know as a Customer Director while customers hung on your every word for €300 per hour and wrote down your recommendations as unique added value. If you were lucky, you sometimes even made it to the press when your client quoted your truth in some trade magazine.

"Because she promised me never to talk about it. She was allowed to import some of my hard disks for free. I've never heard Sonja scream like that before. Diana did, by the way, but that's beside the point. I'm now giving Hilde my end-of-year bonus, and that's the end of it." Ed laughed loudly. I perked up my ears.

"If she ever threatens to think about it differently, we may have other options to help her realize the right choice. Let's assume it's under control," said Peter. "We will at least have her flowers delivered this week."

"What is the status of my file now? I think those 2 months should really make a difference. Can we go through the numbers again?" Ed had asked. Then I heard a computer starting up. This started to interest me. I felt tension rising because I knew somewhere that I was going to witness a huge professional secret that would exceed my wildest fantasies. I gently rolled my chair closer to the doorway.

"Look, Hilde's current project is going to be extended for 3 million euros, but that is still unofficial. Formally, this is currently entering a decisive phase where it is not difficult to position yourself on this so that you can add it to your file. If you also organize an internal evening session and, for example, a breakfast session with potential customers around the challenges of outsourcing in the banking sector or something along those lines, then your visibility is indisputable, and you have achieved a very clear lead. The evaluation is done at 12 months, and that applies to everyone. It's a shame if you are out of the running for some time, but if we start making exceptions, the end is over. In short, your case is straight. No one can get in the way of that. Congratulations." A laptop was closed.

"That's nice," Ed said coolly.

My head was buzzing. This was not possible. I decided that this must be a pure fabrication on my part, something I had heard completely wrong, which was a manifestation of my perverse mind. However, part of Ed's reality would prove equally hallucinatory a few months later.

An email appeared on my screen: "You Won eBay Item: Nick Drake Rare & Live (260032733167)."

A few months later, Ed was promoted to Junior Director.

Hilde had taken a seat next to me again. And had started a conversation with Will who was sitting on her left. To my right, a woman of about 50 had been fiddling with her napkin for a long time and quickly gulping down one glass after another. I seemed to remember Tom, our marketing manager, introducing her to me as his wife, Jeannette. That could be true because she was between us. She didn't make any special impression on me. I now noticed that she looked at least 10 years older than our marketing man, who had been involved in an intensive conversation with Sonja. Jeannette probably felt studied by me a little too explicitly. The fidgeting with the napkin stopped. She turned her face in my direction and raised her eyes pointedly at me as the opening lines flashed through her mind. I decided not to give her hope and asked Youri to pass me the white wine again, after which I simply refilled my glass while Jeannette placed her hand on the foot of the empty glass in front of her.

We had new wine, and we stayed in the Burgundy region. A 1984 Montrachet has now been donated. The bouquet was intense and delicate, with a faint almond scent. The temperature was perfect. I started to feel light-headed. For enthusiasts, there was also an Aloxe Corton Premier Cru from 1989 available, but I decided to stick with the white tonight.

Jeannette's fidgeting started again. It got on my nerves.

I saw how Ed had struck up a conversation with the top official. Apparently, the alcohol had also done some work for him because his deathly pale face had actually acquired some color, and the man also appeared to be able to laugh, or at least did his best by regularly folding the corners of his mouth and showing out a few whoppers of teeth stitches. Sonja had a chat with Jodie, Alex's wife, who, for some reason, were not sitting next to each other as a couple. Sonja, how could that woman live with a guy like Ed? It completely escaped me, and time and time again, it made me feel powerless. It defied all logic. No, she knew nothing about my perverse fantasies that Ed had put into practice with Hilde and Diana, but she herself was a victim of one of the most lurid dramas I could imagine and of which I could not see how the word 'forgiveness' or a real attempt to implement it could prevent a rift in their relationship.

The door flew open, the force of the handle striking a star in the glass of my office.

"Harry. What should I do? She is dead. Dead to death." Ed stood sweaty in front of me on a sweltering summer evening in August almost a year ago.

It took a moment for the content of Ed's sentence to sink in. My first reflex was to think of his mother.

"Fuck Harry, I don't know how we can solve this. Sonja is going to kill me. Say something.!"

In my opinion, the death of Ed's mother would not be a reason to kill Ed, or it would be the first mother-in-law to achieve that honor. Suddenly, I knew.

"Rose.? What happened to Rose?"

I felt nauseous. This could not and should not be true.

Although Ed had clearly lost control and seemed clumsy, it seemed to be an expression of frustration for something that had not gone exactly as he had planned rather than sadness and pure despair over the loss of his 1.5-year-old daughter.

"Where is she? What happened, and where is Sonja?" My questions certainly did not answer Ed's request, but I was currently too confused and affected to be able to take or propose any action.

"She's in my car. Down in the parking lot."

I put my hands over my eyes.

"Sonja had to go to a meeting in London this morning and left early by plane. I took them to the airport, along with Rose, who I then had to take to daycare. I forgot. She probably fell asleep, so I didn't notice anything when I got here. I wanted to drive home, and then, I found her."

I got up, spun on my legs, and walked to the toilet. I washed my face and hands. I hoped not to find anyone when I returned to my office, which would confirm that my psychological condition would be definitively labeled 'deadly ill,' after which I would voluntarily report to a psychiatric institution for a month-long treatment.

Ed stood motionless in my office with little sign of emotion. I now also had sweat pouring down my forehead.

"So, Harry, how do we solve this?"

"Goddammit, how do we solve this? Man, what are you talking about? I don't understand what your question is. What can be solved? Rose is dead, and there is no way to find out. We will call the police and a doctor, and then you can tell your story again. Furthermore, Sonja should be contacted, but I leave it up to you to determine the tactics. You should know what is best. Although this whole situation actually makes me think you understand the fuck out of it."

That last comment was below the belt, but I couldn't resist. Ed didn't respond to my statement, so he went to get coffee and started fiddling with his cell phone.

The funeral was dramatic. I will never forget the white casket at the altar. Ed and Sonja moved like wax figures that day. Little to no emotion, which I believe was the result of a heavy dose of tranquilizers. Instead of taking a period of leave with Sonja, Ed was more present than ever at Value Creators Inc. The whole affair had, in fact, passed without much impact. There was never any mention of it in the office after that funeral, and Ed no longer referred to Rose and the tragedy that had occurred. Julie and I still talked about it regularly. Especially now that Julie had been pregnant for more than 2 months, the horror of Rose and the images of the funeral were regularly discussed. Usually, we expressly mention our own happiness. More than 6 months ago, at a reception, I asked Ed how Sonja was actually doing after the presentation of some customer concert organized by Value Creators. That was my somewhat clumsy way of broaching the topic without daring to mention the entire event by name explicitly.

Ed had reacted strangely because there was apparently no relationship between my comment and the misery that had affected them, making my question about Sonja's condition inexplicable and inappropriate. Since then, I, too, had kept quiet. Rose was dead. A little girl of 1.5 years old, strapped into a maxi cozy seat in the back seat of a Land Rover Discovery, helplessly exposed to scorching heat for 10 hours, temperatures above 40°C. Dehydrated to death. She was buried in a white lacquered oak coffin. Flowers on it. A giant wreath of white roses from Value Creators Inc. expressed our sincere condolences. Drove out of the church on wheels. Then, into the ground. Literally and figuratively, sand over it.

The fidgeting with the napkin next to me disturbed my thoughts. I realized that I hadn't seen Sonja since that funeral. Radiant and relaxed, she sat next to her Ed, talking to Tom. My glass was empty again. Hilde was now talking to Youri, who was laughing. That was something new for me. My glass was refilled, and I downed it in one gulp. There was a relaxed atmosphere at the table with chatter, laughter, laughter, and the sound of cutlery and glasses. Pressure on the bladder made me decide to look for a toilet in Will's castle. When

I stood up, my head started to spin. The champagne and wine had done their job properly.

The toilet was at the back of a long corridor that was only dimly lit. Feeling my way, because I was no longer feeling fresh on my feet, I moved towards the door, grabbed the handle, and was blinded by the light that turned on automatically. Once I got used to the bright light, I saw a pale man with red-shot eyes and enormous rings of perspiration around his armpits. A white shirt would have spared me better than this light blue one. The chamois would not have held up. That was the first time, as far as I could remember. So far, my mother's intervention had caused me a lot of discomfort, as the stitching in my shirts felt extremely uncomfortable, but the results had been good so far. I took a pee, flushed, and turned on the tap to wash my hands. With enormous force, the water sprayed through the white enamel of the sink onto my crotch, where a huge, dark, wet spot emerged. God damn that too! Now, one more or less wet spot wouldn't make a difference. I dabbed some on my pants with the towel, dried my hands, and left the toilet. Somehow, I made a mistake when walking back to the garden doors because suddenly, I found myself standing in front of a closed door at the end of a corridor. Instead of turning around, I lowered the handle to open the door. The kitchen was huge, with a large island in the middle. A 6-burner gas stove, as well as a separate grill and a deep fryer. Smeg everywhere represented. Only now did I see her sitting at a desk in the kitchen corner under the dim light.

"Uh. Sorry, I took the wrong door," I apologized.

The hostess put what looked like a smile on her face.

"That's OK. Now I'll see someone again." It now dawned on me that I had hardly seen Harriette at the table all evening.

"You're Harry, aren't you?"

I was surprised by her comment. Despite the vacant, disinterested impression she had made when Will had introduced me to her, my name and appearance had stuck in her mind.

"Yes, I'm Harry. I'd say drenched Harry," I said while pointing to my shirt and pants.

The glass of whiskey was brought to his mouth with trembling hands. The opened bottle of Chevis Regal only contained a small amount of alcoholic liquid at the bottom.

"I don't know you, Harry, but I'm curious if you know what 'the end of life' means."

At the end of life, she spoke slowly and articulately. Little Rose flashed through my mind. Apparently, it wasn't really the intention for a dialogue to develop between us. Harriette gave me her comprehensive and thoughtful definition of the end of life.

"Gaining a sense of time.

I'm not getting a kiss in the morning anymore.

Faking an orgasm every week."

I thought about Marc and Joan.

".Being completely ignored by your husband for over 10 years.

Having to accept one slip-up after another blindly.

Downing a bottle of whiskey every day to ease the pain.

Go to the plastic surgeon at least twice a year at your husband's appointment."

She grabbed her breasts with her right hand. Then, she handed me the bottle of whiskey and continued her monologue. I downed the remaining whiskey in one gulp.

"Wake up with a deep desire to go to sleep.

Being a hostess to your own husband.

Devouring books to avoid thinking about your own reality."

To my amazement, she read all this off a paper she held in her right hand.

"Do you understand me?" she said hopefully after she had put the tray back on the desk to signify that she was done.

"Eeuuuuuuuh." I felt physically uncomfortable, not only because of the topic of conversation but also because of the alcohol that started to manifest itself in my entire body.

"Euuuh. Yes, I think I understand you. It's like starting to live or stopping wetting your bed."

Harriette frowned.

This person is crazy, I thought. I suddenly didn't feel like dealing with Mrs. Will anymore. I have to get out of here.

"Good evening." The hallway turned before my eyes.

"Why are you running away? Come back!!" it chased me from the kitchen.

As I stood on the threshold that gave access to the garden, gasping for air and feeling the sweat trickling down between my shoulder blades, I burst out laughing. The whole table was looking at me. It went black before my eyes for a second, and I saw stars. I grabbed the door frame as my eyes tried to focus on the company.

Will was the only one standing with a raised glass, gesturing in my direction. I started to hear words through the ringing in my ears.

"Spensers. 15 million Euro. Sweating."

My legs felt loose from my body, and I thought I was being controlled like a puppet as my body moved to my place, where I plopped down in my chair between Hilde and Jeannette. Several of my tablemates applauded as they stared at me. My glass was refilled, which felt good as I let the white grape juice slide down the back of my throat.

"Now, let's face it, wouldn't any of us just piss our pants out of sheer enthusiasm at such a deal." Hilarity everywhere. The fidgeting with the napkin that I noticed out of the corner of my right eye started to get on my nerves again.

"But, come on, Harry, say something now. What is your secret to shaping and closing such a deal? What is the secret of your sweat glands?" Roar as Will utters these last words.

"Speech. Speech. Speech." echoed through my ears.

Speech. They all went up the tree! I took the bottle of white wine, and as the sudden shout of 'Oooooooooooh' reached me, I stood up. Everyone should do this, I thought as my lips closed around the bottleneck of the Montrachet 1984, and the golden liquid flowed inside.

"Fuck, stop that annoying fidgeting of yours!" I shouted as I grabbed the napkin from her hands and threw it across the table. Jeannette looked at me in horror and started to sob.

"Jesus Christ, man, are we going to fucking cry about a napkin being launched. I'm sorry, so please STOP," I roared.

Laughter and commotion had now given way to an eerie silence.

"Hey Harry, you're drunk. Let's keep it reasonable." The words came from Ed, who had lifted himself out of his chair to address me. Mister Responsibility.

"Of course, I'm drunk, just like everyone else here. And, no, I don't feel like keeping it reasonable. It's a good thing to be able to be unreasonable sometimes. The truth isn't always reasonable, Ed. You should know that better than anyone."

"Harry, be sensible," Hilde muttered next to me, "you might want to go home."

Her hand slipped from my left wrist.

Ed was red in the face and glared at me.

"Harry, you are drunk. Your eyes look so strange," Ed said forcefully.

"What would you like? That I had a strange look out of my ass or something."

It must be said I remained shrewd despite the hour and the alcohol content in my blood.

"Listen, buddy," I said while waving my right index finger in Ed's direction. "You really need to keep your mouth shut because even when sober, you are capable of doing the most horrible things as long as it is in line with your never to stop career. And don't ask me to go into details because that could upset you here at this table, along with your wife, Hilde, and Diana, among others. I suggest that they put their heads together after this feast."

Diana now joined the discussion while Ed looked at me in amazement.

"What are you talking about?" she screamed at me.

"You know that very well. It is certainly not a secret at all for everyone around the table except for that shroud next to you. Do I really have to draw a picture of it? That scream of yours is familiar to many here! Luckily not me!"

"Ooooh, Harry has to do this now," Hilde whispered desperately.

"No, of course, you don't HAVE to do this, but it is sometimes good to dot the I's and cross the I's. Are 'transparency' and 'respect for the individual' not part of the core values of Value Creators Inc? I don't understand who could have a problem with my comments. Ok, I drank a little too much white wine, which was of an unprecedented class, by the way, Will, but that doesn't change the truth."

I now turned to Will, who was staring in my direction with his mouth open.

"Listen, Will, the Spensers deal is a non-existent deal that I seriously doubt will ever come off, so spare yourself the euphoria and me the pressure disguised as pats on the back! Spensers is a first-class prick and not interested in that bastard of ours. We're not going to lose that to the paving stones here. HR outsourcing to Eastern European countries, do you believe it yourself?!"

Instead of a response from Will, my attention was again drawn to Diana, who was interpellated by her top official but completely ignored it and barked at me: "Don't you dare. Do you really think you would have a chance with me?"

My roar of laughter faded into nothingness.

Alex introduced himself to the altercation from an unexpected source. "I agree, those Eastern Europeans are just causing a nuisance here. All that rubbish. And no respect for our language or culture."

I didn't wait for the end of his sentence.

"Where do you get the illusion that I feel the need to be seduced and degraded into a ride, Diana? Sorry, my midlife crisis may be hitting me hard, but not to that level! Lady Di, you'd better pay some attention to your top official because the gentleman doesn't look very happy tonight if you ask me.

"Oooh, please, Lloyd, say something," Diana breathed to her husband.

The top official was indeed given an identity. He sat up and coughed loudly.

Ed had now sunk back into his chair.

"At least tell them how much I look like Diana!" she begged her husband. Lloyd wisely remained silent.

A weak laugh now took possession of me. "Do you know that Lady Di left us a long time ago? Ask your Lloyd if he wants to chase you through that Parisian tunnel at 180 an hour. It will inevitably be a lot more exciting than your current life as a couple. What are you,

Lloyd? And I would change that title from Director Public Sector to Director Public Sector because."

"OK, now it's fucking beautiful." Youri's arm closed like a clamp around my neck. I couldn't produce anything more than a pathetic murmur.

I struggled and squirmed, but all I managed was that my blue Ralph Lauren shirt came loose from my body as Alex dragged me along the gravel path to the parking lot. A dark blue soaked shirt with sleeves lifted in the grass in front of me was the last thing I saw as I was lifted into my car by Alex.

"Could you also have a car declared a 'total loss' from the inside? Could you, as a human being, have it declared a 'total loss'?"

I opened the door and sat for a moment with my eyes closed, becoming aware of the morning, the smell of dew on the freshly mown fields, the song of the thrush announcing that the eggs had been laid and breeding had begun.

It was 5:50 AM. I hadn't slept for a long time. I felt remarkably fresh, considering the amount of alcohol I had consumed. It looked like I had also spewed up the greatest misery during the night. Wondering why I was only wearing my undershirt, I pulled myself out of the car, stood up, shook my head, and grabbed the damp spot in my crotch. I had really pissed my fucking pants. I couldn't stray much deeper into my most banal being.

My thoughts turned to the evening and night that had passed. My god, things had really gone wrong. I fully realized that I had gone terribly over the line without every detail sinking in. Yet, it was a sense of pride that I experienced rather than embarrassment or regret.

Last night's phone call with Julie played through my mind, and as we replayed our conversation, I felt a blissful warmth inside that was more than helpful in my current state. I was looking forward to going home. However, driving home now would be fatal. My blood must still be fermenting from all the alcohol, and I didn't want to risk losing my driver's license because that would mean losing the key to my cocoon.

"Hey, good morning. I love you! Everything is OK. I'll be home soon. Call me if you want." I looked up Julie's name in my file and forwarded the text.

The air was already sweltering, and the sun was shining. My footsteps caused small dust puffs in the loose sand that climbed up my ankle to my shin and calf. My head pounded. The serenity of this early morning, the still life around me, and the peace clashed with the chaos that my life had become. The images from the night before flashed through my mind again. My God. I seriously messed up. I had behaved like a drunk teenager and had literally and figuratively disappeared from the scene, waving around me, actually, not even of free will. I remembered Youri, probably the only one in a sober state, who had grabbed me by the collar and shouted that it had to be over. I had gotten through my tirade, had said everything I wanted to say, had hurt enough people, and it had been nice. My blue shirt soaked in the grass, a final witness to my debauchery. Value Creators Inc. could soon be without Jones. That was clear. Would Value Creators suffer anything from that? Would I suffer anything from it?!

The road I followed made a slight bend to the right. A little further on, a sandy path led into a bush.

Gaining a sense of time, it suddenly flashed through my mind. I couldn't quite remember the other definitions except that they were all related to Harriette's relationship with Will, or lack thereof. It was a beautiful and apt description of the concept of 'the end of life.' I was reminded of the time when, as a 9-year-old, I was dropped off at my uncle's farm for a 2-week holiday. I loved the farm life, but I was overcome by enormous homesickness every evening. Of course, I already had a limited sense of time, and it was precisely because I knew how long those 14 days would last that every night was so difficult. 14 nights, 13 nights, 12 more nights. It seemed endless. My parents were traveling abroad. My brother was staying with friends, and I was stuck here. There was no way out. That awareness, in combination with the intensity of my homesickness, apparently unleashed a creativity in me that allowed me to manipulate the concept of time. Being able to replace the word 'pas' with 'already' seemed to be revolutionary, and it had an equally great impact on my experience of that same time, of those same 14 days. On Tuesday morning, I woke up realizing that if I realized that it was 'already' Tuesday (and tomorrow is already Wednesday., and then it's already Thursday!) instead of 'just,' the world would be a very different place.

Finitude, or the consciousness thereof, had everything to do with the sense of time. Nowadays, I can no longer use that 'trick' in the opposite direction. The word 'pass' no longer occurred in my experience, whether it was pleasant or less pleasant moments. I could no longer 'activate' it. The time train went faster and faster. If you have completely lost control at the age of 38 and every 10 years seems like a second, what must that feel like at the age of 75? I will ask my father about that next time.

I had taken the forest path. I realized that my search for any traces of deer or other game was pointless when I became aware of a wide tire track that ran the entire route in front of me. Oaks, beeches, and birches adorned either side of the forest path I strolled through. I thought back to the years when I used to sneak through forests at dawn, guided by my father, hoping to catch foxes, deer, or badgers. Every confrontation with an animal was, time and time again, an intense experience that I could enjoy for a long time. My father and I never exchanged many words; it would only scare the animals away, but the intensity of the moment, the experience, and the time together were indescribable and unforgettable. The forest path bends slightly to the left at the end. I decided to walk a little further before turning around and going back to my car. Fatigue struck. The light rustling of the leaves, supplemented by some chattering of early birds, provided a welcome break from the pure silence. When I reached the bend about 100 meters further and cast my gaze into the dark avenue, my breath caught in my throat. The tire track had veered abruptly to the right, and the dark red Porsche had wrapped itself almost completely around the tree. From films, I remembered head-on collisions or accidents with torn wreckage, torn bodies, organs, and body parts thrown away, and seas of blood. The reality for me, however, was more hallucinatory precisely because of the complete absence of outward signs of the crash, which had occurred with such violence that it seemed as if the tree had been planted afterward in the center of the steel. A modern abstract work of art, 'Earth meets Steel.'

Up close, I saw her head leaning against the tree as if in a deep sleep. The nose and left eye socket hung asymmetrically in the face, so you could see that it was not quite right. Other than that, she looked peaceful. I saw the piece of crumpled paper between her right hand

and a piece of twisted dashboard; deeply longing to go to sleep, I could just about read.

OPTIONS II

Unbelievable that more than 50 years ago, the 'untouchables,' the lowest caste in India, had to move around like this all day long, erasing their own footprints so that no evidence of their presence was left behind. Although the Indian Constitution has formally banned 'untouchability' since 1950, in reality, Dalits are still without rights. It was in a book by Norman Lewis, in which he lets the reader become part of his travels through India that I had read a chapter about it, and I was reminded of it now, at 3:00 with a hangover, I crawled backward out of Sam's bedroom head on hands and knees. It gradually became a daily ritual for me, but my cursing would be in stark contrast to the satisfied resignation with which the 'untouchables' faced their fate. In addition, crawling through mud and shit was something different than crawling over the heated 'quick step' that covered the floor in the children's rooms. Still, I cursed my boys, especially the existence of pacifiers. Perhaps the pet, particularly the dog, would soon lose out to this mouth plug. Sam had no fewer than 7 in different colors, not one the same, and no clear favorite either. That depended a bit on his mood. Neither Sam nor Ben had understood that by simply exploring their bed, they could easily regain possession of that wonderful surrogate nipple. That they could get the game back in their mouth with one movement with their fist, saving everyone a lot of misery, especially for Daddy. Instead, the loss of the 'tute' was always responded to with a hysterical screaming match that only stopped when Julie or I put a pacifier in the mouth. When the boys were still real babies, and the cot was on Julie's side next to our bed, it was an almost natural movement to immediately put the plug back between the lips with a fist bump when starting to cry. With that, we dug our own graves. The men went to their own room after 4 months, and the supply of teats grew steadily. So these days, the process was this: screeching, being woken up (either by myself or an elbow bump from Julie), sneaking out of bed and trying to avoid any toys, tiptoeing to the bed of the deeply sad son for whom the end of the world had presented itself; looking for a pacifier; controlling myself by internally channeling all the curses that came to mind; plug in the plug and stroke the man's head until his breathing became deep and slow, as a sign that sleep was gaining the upper hand again; sneak back out of the room; into bed and try to continue sleeping. However, this process had an unpleasant variant if the returned teat was not the favorite of the moment. Sam wasn't going to be fooled by a 'Pacifier.' If it wasn't the 'real thing,' my retreat into a backward frog position was rudely interrupted by new whining or roaring. Since there was little to no logic behind the choice of the favorite teat, after all, the taste cannot be disputed, I used a 'Trial and Error' principle, knowing that with seven teats, there was a statistically high chance of being interrupted again.

Tonight, I was lucky. Sam went straight to sleep. However, I couldn't sleep anymore. After 15 minutes of tossing and turning, I turned to Julie, kissed her forehead, stroked her slightly rounded belly, and carefully slid out of bed. The severity of the situation at Value Creators Inc. and the resulting need to seriously consider alternatives kept me awake.

Half past three. In the living room, I selected John Mellencamp's 'Lonesome Jubilee,' a masterful album from 1989 that was full of American folk rock songs. With a glass of Côte du Rhône Village in hand, I settled into the sofa and took out my 'Options' magazine. The opening notes of 'Paper in Fire' came to me through the speakers.

The situation had changed, or at least there were a number of implications following the barbecue that made my options list less premature. At least, that's what you would have expected after my 'act.'

Write a book. Could I actually do that, and what on earth would the theme be? Of course, I could open up a number of stories about life behind the scenes at Value Creators Inc., but that would be considered defamation, so that wasn't really a possibility. A book about my own life would not be very exciting, and the stuff about my adolescent behavior that might, with some imagination, be interesting for a few adolescents was too embarrassing for me. Imagine that acquaintances of mine, including Julie, would also happen to leaf through that book because they had received it for free and for the sake of decency, they took a look through it (you have to encourage a friend!), then their image of the Harry Jones they knew would have to be drastically adjusted, and not in a positive way. Another option could be to write fiction based on a few basic elements from my private and professional life. A 'Faction' or 'Auto-Fiction,' as it were, starting from some basic factual data such as my job as a consultant and current family situation, supplemented and interspersed with all kinds of exciting and silly situations. I tried, without much success, to imagine it in concrete terms. Besides, I would lack writing talent and patience, two critical success factors for completing a manuscript. It must have been fantastic to be able to hold your own written story in your hands. Yet, it was something very concrete and tangible, which I often missed in my job. In fact, there was very little tangible in my current working environment. I had a lot of my own fault for that. How could spending hours driving around in the car listening to your favorite top 100 lead to anything tangible? I simply wasn't able to communicate, build, and maintain relationships at the moment, which automatically meant that no new concrete deals were realized. Anyway, looking back on my career, which can objectively be called successful and which had generated quite a bit of turnover for Value Creators, I could now think of nothing, not a single recommendation, that had been effectively implemented. Although I had recently become aware, encouraged by my armpits, of my dissatisfaction and discomfort with my current functioning, this observation was now very confronting. That called for a glass of wine!

Nick Hornby was an example of a successful writer who knew how to write realistic fiction. Whether the books were deliberately written with a movie audience in mind was not so important. The fact was that the good man wrote bestsellers, almost all of which were made into films with A-list actors in the leading roles. That meant a cash register! No, that would not have been given to me, discouraging me a bit. Mellencamp was now singing about 'too many people with empty hands' (the instrumental intermezzo at 1 minute 52 is masterful). I might be able to whip up a raunchy porn book, I thought, hopefully. It was certain that with my sexual fantasies, it would be possible to write an entertaining book of about 200 pages. And just imagine if it was made into a movie starring John Leslie and Traci Lord. I could just imagine the scenes with the food. The pudding, the strawberries with whipped cream. The scene with the cucumber However, I wondered how the scene with the Lilliputian, the 2-meter-tall black woman, the two nuns, the coconuts, and that champagne bottle would be depicted. Maybe I could play a cameo role in it. Wow, that would be the first porn movie I would buy. My enthusiasm and excitement were nipped in the bud by thoughts of Julie, family, and friends. First of all, they wouldn't like their friend the porn author ("My husband? Eeeuh, that's a celebrated author. What genre? Well, porn. That's a genre with mechanical intimacy. Aah, you're a connoisseur."). In addition, they might also start asking serious questions about my private life, with only the wrong conclusions: My friends would think that day in and day out, I only walked around in a loose bathrobe with my rock-hard erection underneath constantly at the ready, waiting for the redeeming moment of my bathrobe falling open at the sight of a pair of shapely buttocks. Buttocks of my Julie, but in the belief and imagination of my friends and other women.

And in Julie's eyes? She knew all too well that I hated walking around in bathrobes and always laughed at me for my un-sexy night outfits. Not to mention rock-hard erections and cucumbers. So Julie's thoughts would be fed that I would have all kinds of perverse illusions that I could only express with other women. So, it is a disastrous story for rediscovering blind trust between the spouses.

I certainly didn't want to imagine the thoughts of my family. Author? I wasn't sure.

The job of 'key maker,' second on my shortlist, was certainly not an obvious choice, but a number of elements continued to fascinate me. Key makers that I knew existed, such as my friend who had made the keys for the Bertone, worked very individualistically, sometimes even quite lonely, in their shop, often no more than 15 m² tucked away in some anonymous shopping center. They had their radios on and received not so many customers but keys, which were handed over quickly by the owners without too many words. While the owner disappeared into the day to deal with more important matters, the key maker got to work with the milling machine and a piece of steel to shape a new suitable key. Being completely alone, without too much interruption, communication limited to a minimum, listening to a radio or a playlist, and working on a concrete, tangible product. These were all parts that I particularly liked at the moment.

At Value Creators, everything was based on teamwork, over-communication, and, in my opinion, little added value.

Considering those specific key maker traits, I was the key maker for Value Creators Inc. for a while. Since I hardly communicated anymore, I listened to music all day long, whether or not driving around. OK, tangible or intangible results hadn't been there for a while, but that didn't seem to matter much after all.

I also liked the aspect of 'Limited Creativity.' That was actually a quality whose absence made me suspect that authorship would not be for me. And where plagiarism is disastrous for a writer, it is precisely a very important point for the key maker. He is concerned with that perfect copy for the key to the front door, the cellar, the laundry room, the wine cellar, the bedroom, the nunnery, the 'stay away from my body' house, the partner club, etc. In short, the key maker implicitly held 'the key' that provided access to the key owners' most intimate 'places'. Perhaps he never physically visited all those locations himself, or perhaps he had to take the plunge with that 25-year-old nun or that dancer from that swingers' club. Changing locks may have resulted in interesting 'relocations' where you could peek into a complete stranger's home undisturbed and be allowed into your private world. Yes, it is likely that Harry Jones is also a real voyeur. But you might wonder, 'Who isn't,' judging by the endless stream of reality shows and their enormous success. Nowadays, the entire media is focused on all kinds of 'formats' that allow people to be seen in all their animality, with the urge for exhibitionism among the participants leading to situations that would embarrass animals. What do you mean by norms and values?

However, the dexterity of the key makers with their hands and machines did scare me. The slightest 'do it yourself' job in the house was unceremoniously outsourced by Julie to some entrepreneur listed in the Golden Pages. Julie was unrelenting about this: I was no longer allowed to do anything at home except ironing and cooking, two household chores that should not be underestimated and which I had mastered more than adequately. However, I could not be blamed for lacking commitment or goodwill, but it must be said that all kinds of jobs were not given to me. For years, Julie supported my frantic attempts to carry out minor repairs (is replacing a lamp actually a repair.?) and interior improvements with my own hands, usually. This probably arose from a belief that certain activities, which fall neatly within traditional gender roles, are preferably performed by men because it caresses their male mega ego and thus nourishes the feeling that they are indispensable. Julie may be a child psychiatrist, but in this case, she had made a truly wrong diagnosis (but preferably with me than with innocent children, as this saves them from a serious error of judgment, and it is undoubtedly also to my advantage that Julie still does not fully understand me has) for two reasons; First of all, any do-it-yourself activity is a no-brainer for me as I hate it so much. Secondly, role models also leave me completely indifferent, which does not alter the fact that the man and the woman each have their own place within the relationship. I am also honest enough to admit that the majority of the tasks, activities, and responsibilities within my relationship are borne by Julie; as far as I am concerned, we do not need to discuss that. Much to the annoyance of Julie, who regularly presents my balance sheet and, it must be said, it doesn't look that great. Apart from ironing mountains of laundry, which should not be underestimated and confirms that I don't care about being a role model and cooking, my role is mainly limited to bringing in significant sums of money that disappear into nothing. Since our very first meeting, Julie and I have one joint account that we draw from every month as if we had won the lotto. We never argue about money. At the end of the month, we find that we are in the red again and start the next day in a good mood again. Is one pot wet a bottomless pit? Indeed, but in our case, it is certainly never a source of marital strife.

Another, and certainly not unimportant, reason for my unemployment regarding DIY activities is the complete lack of competencies and patience to bring these kinds of 'shitty jobs' to a good or acceptable conclusion. Ultimately, Julie came to that conclusion herself in a confrontational manner. We just moved into our new 45m² apartment, which was a huge step forward after our first 20m² loft, where we had lasted 6 years together. We couldn't afford more and were very proud and happy about it. Julie's dog, Candy, loved it too. Candy was not a stray dog that had happened to wander in or an emaciated one that had been left tied to a post by its owner and, in its sad, neglected condition, had aroused Julie's pity. I might have been able to accept that. No, after 7 years together, Julie had the bright idea, fully aware of my deep aversion to dogs, to test our relationship by purchasing a 2-month-old cocker spaniel, Candy. The threat of 'get the dog out or get me out' was completely ignored by the child psychiatrist, which meant that I spent one evening shivering under a raincoat in my Ford Fiesta. Candy was a sweet dog, and the proverbial 'get some fresh air' with her did me good. However, it remained a dog; of course, she couldn't do anything about that, but it still bothered me. Julie was extremely satisfied with the results of our relationship test. She didn't know at that moment that I also had a few tests up my sleeve, listening to the code names Agnes, Denise, and Muna. Once we moved into our apartment, we tried to make something practical and cozy out of it. Some of our travel photos were enlarged and mounted on the wall. Besides a few too many holes, loose filler here and there, and photo frames at an interesting angle, nothing suggested that my DIY skills were below par. Julie also thought there was something wrong with it. Not everything was straight (Once I finally settled with my permission to carry out chores myself, this turned out to be a pure lie). My bigger challenge was attaching a pull-out clothes rack in the bathroom and our velour curtains in the area we proudly called our living room. I had taken a full day off to complete these two tough tasks. To allow me to carry out the activities with utmost concentration and undisturbed, Candy was outsourced to friends for a day.

The laundry rack that I purchased consisted of an ingenious system that saved space and was particularly handy according to the packaging. The confirmation was also extremely simple because it was on a small piece of paper, postcard size, summarized in 2 drawings that spoke for themselves, which could not be said of the Chinese text underneath. I started the business with complete confidence. It must be said I had the device installed in just 45 minutes. With a click, you could disconnect one section of the rack, pull it out, attach it to the hooks I had attached to the other side of the bathroom, and string up the clotheslines. When you were in the bath, the lines ran above your head, and you could easily pull your towel down. I thought as if I admired the result. Attaching the curtains was a completely different matter. Hanging curtain rails at a height of 4.5 meters with a ladder of 1.80 meters is quite a challenge, even if you are quite tall like me. Our ceilings were particularly beautiful and somewhat of our showpiece as the moldings and the parquet gave the apartment a special cachet. The curtains had to be attached to the street side where, in an extension, there was a huge window measuring 2 by 3.5 meters.

This bay window hung like a covered balcony about 7 meters above the street. I pushed our desk up to the start of the extension, placed the steps on top, and climbed up with my drill in my clammy hands. When I looked down, I saw the cars speeding beneath me. It was a perilous operation that I experienced as playing a game of Russian roulette on my own. With the drill running, I fell slightly forward, aiming for the dot I had just scratched on the wall with a pencil. The table wobbled under my weight and the power tour that was being performed. Miraculously, I managed to get it off without a scratch, and after all the holes had been filled with plugs, I screwed the rails in. Then I threaded in the curtains. My job was done. In the evening, while Candy barked loudly and enthusiastically, Julie admired the fruits of my hard work. This was celebrated with a bout of heavy sex where our whimpering exceeded that of Candy, who was locked in the toilet for the occasion.

The next morning, I was enjoying the bath. I included the Q Special edition Joy Division. While reading the description of their concert on January 11, 1980, of which there is a very bad bootleg under the name 'Desperation Takes Hold,' I was startled by a hellish noise in which I recognized a combination of falling materials, screaming followed by cursing from Julie and Candy whining. Thoughts raced through my head, looking for possible disaster scenarios that had just happened in the living room. The cursing came closer, as did the footsteps and the tapping of dog paws on the parquet. The door flew open. Julie was yelling at me with a broken curtain rail in her hand. Candy was crazy, excited by the enormous noise of the loose curtain rails and Julie's verbal violence; she jumped into the bath on top of me. I reflexively rose, my Q sliding into the water as I grabbed a towel on the clothesline.

The clothes rack came loose when the dog was in the bath, shaking the water from her fur. I saw it happen when I pulled off my towel. Julie didn't notice anything because she was still shouting and ranting at me in a blind rage. Suddenly, the rack shot completely out of the wall and was catapulted to the other side. "Bend down," I shouted. The blow was enormous. One of the plugs drilled into Candy with the screw at her temple. The beast gave one roar of pain before sliding beneath the water.

Later that day, she died at the vet, who could not have done anything about it. She was only 9 months old, which is not enough in dog years. Julie and I survived this event, although my friend initially suggested that she would never forgive me. In a way, in my opinion, it was actually her reward for the trick she had done to me by purchasing Candy in the first place. Since then, I have no longer been expected to lift a finger when it comes to manual tasks. I'm simply forbidden. So, when it comes to the practical side of the key-making profession, that's probably where the shoe pinches for me.

"Hey daddy"

Ben unexpectedly stood in front of me. 5 A.M.

"Can't you sleep anymore, buddy? It's still a bit early."

He nestled on my lap and wrapped both his arms around my neck.

"Dad, I had a night nightmare. He had a long beard and came out of the woods to eat Sam. Dad, he was mean, that night owl."

I ruffled his hair. "Try to sleep, little man; the night owl must have a huge stomach ache from such a huge piece of Sam. I think he has gone back into the woods to go to sleep after his heavy meal."

"But I want to go see which part of Sam is left." Not smart, I thought. The nightmare that had eaten a piece of my son would not really be conducive to Ben's peaceful night's sleep. Luck was on my side because while I diligently looked for creative solutions, I felt Ben's calm breathing on my neck and his arms limp around me. I carefully placed him on the couch, where he slept peacefully. Mellencamp had finished singing. It became light outside, and birds began to appear. Another 2.5 hours before I had to leave the house.

After the 'Lonesome Jubilee,' it was time for Ed Kuepper's 'Honey Steel's Gold.' The former singer of the Saints released a new solo album in 1990, in which he constantly balanced subdued acoustic sounds and guitar violence. In addition to catchy pop songs, 'Honey Steel's Gold' also produces a number of pure atmospheric songs, such as the 9-minute opening track 'Kings of Voice,' which evokes an oppressive mood through the combination of a subtle drum rhythm and a simple but moving piano melody.

I wondered if Will had already had the keys to his house replaced by a keymaker to lock himself in and prevent Harriette's spirit from entering. As a key maker, would you also see the naked truth within that castle? What would Will be up to now, around 6:30 in the morning? He lay on the bed in his boxer shorts with Harriette's shawl wrapped around his wrist against his nose, smelling the scent of his wife, staring at the ceiling with tears streaming down his cheeks. Or would he sleep peacefully, dreaming of the next big deal? He lay exhausted, sleeping next to a beauty who was at least 15 years younger, who reinforced his feeling that Harriette could never have been happy and that it was just as well, initially for himself. And easier. Did he have a guilt complex, a fear complex, an anger complex, or no complex at all

"Listen, Jones," he started the Monday after the barbecue when I reported to his office after he summoned me. "You know that based on your behavior last Saturday, I can and must immediately dismiss you. And I can do that without you being able to drag anything out of the deal because this is a deliberate mistake, and it doesn't matter how long you've worked for us or what your track record is. I assume that you no longer want to be among your colleagues."

That was interesting. After hearing my story in general terms, Julie's first reaction was that I should feel extremely ashamed and very uncomfortable at the thought of seeing my colleagues again, let alone working with them. But honestly, that feeling was completely missing. Yes, I realized that I had gone too far and that I shouldn't expect to work at Value Creators Inc. to be welcomed with open arms, which did not mean that I felt any shame about it. I had had the feeling all weekend that I had entered a twilight zone, and that was partly due to my own physical state and the awareness of my own behavior, but especially because of the event with Harriette and Will's behavior and statements after hearing the tragic news. But this morning, I went to work without any embarrassment. Will's comment made me realize that Harry Jones, in whose body I lived, no longer reasoned and felt according to the norm.

"Now, of course, I have a practical problem," Will continued his argument.

"Unfortunately, you were the first witness to Harriette's accident; therefore, you know the exact circumstances. I spoke to Tom this morning, and he is now using all his contacts within the media to prevent the press from finding out about this. We have been able to prevent this from being reported in the newspapers today, but we are preparing an article for tomorrow. The funeral is on Wednesday, so this way, we have good control over the communication campaign."

Campaign, I wanted to interrupt him, but I controlled myself.

"It would be extremely inconvenient if there were a potential disruption to reporting. That would raise all kinds of unnecessary questions, which would be of no use to anyone, right, Jones? So I suggest we forget everything, and I mean EVERYTHING, that happened this past weekend. Your completely unacceptable behavior, the incident with Harriette. I will ensure that your performance is kept quiet internally, and I will kick out the first person who reports it."

"And your truth is also being concealed internally, I assume?"

Will's neck veins tensed as his cheeks and ears turned bright red. His fists clenched. However, the man managed to control himself. An important characteristic of a true leader.

"I'm telling you, we're erasing this weekend from our memories. You go back to work. You're just concentrating on that deal with Spensers. I want you to give John an accurate update on that every week. I expect you to come up with a first contract within 2 months at the latest. Otherwise, I'm afraid we'll have another bone to settle. Furthermore, I forbid you from coming to the funeral or speaking to anyone about the event. Did you tie it all up in those shells of yours?"

Not so much knotted, but everything was clear to me. Yet, I also thought that a characteristic of a real leader is being able to explain complex situations clearly as if they were the most normal thing in the world.

"Will, I captured it all well because you explained it very clearly, which I find admirable given your current private circumstances.

Since I can't come to the funeral, I would like to make a recommendation. If you allow me."

Will's hair stood on tiptoes now, anticipating what was to come. Anticipate. Another character trait of a great leader.

"Perhaps it would be a nice tribute if you would read the text of her letter. Quite poetic if you ask me. I think I remember it, so if you have a pen.".

The right fist could not be avoided; in any case, I was too late. My glasses flew through Will's office and landed on the floor 10 feet away with their frames broken. We were done talking.

I didn't like the opportunity offered by Will at all. My options list, which I had drawn up some time ago and carried with me ever since, had taken on a dynamic life. After the disastrous weekend, I thought that my career at Value Creators was over due to my actions without considering that scenario in advance. Due to Harriette's actions, a completely different turn had suddenly taken place. If I had turned around earlier on that deserted dirt road or, even after noticing the tragedy, had not reported anything, I could now have talked to Will about 'Win-Win' situations. Ok, that conversation would have been short-lived, and the content of my 'win' would have been quite limited as it would simply have meant the end of my career at Value Creators for me without some golden handshake. But I had chosen the humane thing, left Julie a message, called the police, and then Will on his cell phone.

At first, there was no response. It was still damn early, and the good man was probably sleeping off his haze. I left four messages before Will called me back. At the same time, the police car arrived.

Since I had been brief about the reason for my calls, I got a Will on the line, which was about to explode because the bastard who had ruined his evening and taunted his colleagues dared to call him out of bed on a Sunday morning. I let him rage quietly while gesticulating; I showed the police officer the location of the accident further in the woods.

"You will suffer the consequences of this for a very long time. Who do you think you are to misbehave like this? You are a gray mini shrimp in a sea full of Tiger prawns; it's time you realize that, Jones. But I fear that will no longer be with us."

A gray mini shrimp. I thought it was quite clever on a Sunday morning after your own barbecue had ended in a banal shouting match and your wife had deliberately crashed herself into a tree.

"Eeuuh! Will. Will. I'm calling you not so much to talk about that wonderful party of yours on Sunday morning but because I have bad news for you."

"Bad news, bad news. I have bad news for you. You can report to me on Monday morning, and we will arrange your departure. Is that understood?"

"Yes, Will, that is understood, but I still have some less good news for you. Your wife, Harriette, was in an accident; she crashed her car into a tree. Will, she's dead. And it looks like, if you ask me, she committed suicide because I had a conversation with her yesterday, and--"

Will interrupted me.

"I knew that bitch of mine was drunk, just like you, by the way! Where is that wreck?" I wondered if he was talking about his car or his wife.

"I'll be there in 10 minutes," Will called and hung up after I gave him the location.

In a British court case, the circumstances would certainly have led to an interrogation to rule out that Harry Jones had anything directly or indirectly to do with the accident. In that same episode, Will would also try to prove my involvement and frame me for the murder. He would suggest that I had sexually assaulted Harriette in the kitchen during the barbecue on the kitchen island. She had struggled, but his frail wife had lost out to this brute, who, to avoid the risk of his victim coming out of confession, had found nothing better than to stage suicide. The reality of this Sunday morning, however, was less complex. A police officer would certainly have let me blow into my bag at some point, but that wasn't even an issue.

Suddenly, the widower stood in front of me. He looked the part, clean shaven, perfectly ironed corduroy with a coarse checked JW Brown shirt on top and his hair, smeared with spectacle cream, combed back tightly. The Waterboot shoes shone in the sun as the ambulance sirens approached.

There was no altercation between me and Will as the 2 officers took care of him immediately. I was not asked anything more, not even what I was doing in this place at this early hour or how I had discovered the tragedy. I started walking slowly back to my car when I heard sirens blaring again. A fire truck came rushing towards me. Probably, sawing had to be done.

When I got to my car, I wiped some debris off my seat with an old newspaper, got behind the wheel, and drove home.

"Harry, you look awful. I've been terribly worried and missing you."

Julie had already showered as she snuggled up to me and wrapped herself in my arms. I smelled her still-wet-washed hair. The smell of apples. That was my love, ready to forgive me, not, as many would do, berating me for my immature behavior.

"Are the children still asleep?"

I looked at the clock, it was 8:45 AM and still silent. Julie nodded in agreement. We sat down on the couch. I laid my head deep in her neck and fell asleep.

My provisional third alternative on the list was that of Chambre d'hôte. There had to be music in it, and maybe this was the moment that would turn that dream into a realistic project. In my opinion, every individual or couple has the idea of starting a Chambre d'hôte. It was the clichéd cliché. And for good reason. There was something sweetly adventurous about it: buying an old 'mas' in the south of France or Umbria on an impulse, selling your house, leaving everything behind, and driving south in a fully packed Volvo Bertone to start a new life of conviviality, good food and drinks, sun-tanned, cheerful customers. It was superficial and profound at the same time, the ideal combination. The conversations during the evening meal, when the wine was flowing freely, could take unexpected intimate turns with no subject being taboo. The next day, the guests left again, each to a different destination, leaving behind no evidence that the conversations had actually taken place or that the insights had contributed anything. I would feel like a fish in water in such a setting:

being able to express my opinion without obligation and making friends for an evening who would all be impressed by my phenomenal cooking skills. During the day, I prepare for that feast. I would unceremoniously throw out annoying guests; my guesthouse has no room for sour souls, arrogant, pretentious people, or bourgeois, frumpy people.

Julie and I would live on love. Ben, Sam, and all those who followed would grow up in a world of harmony where normal people, artists, and eccentrics found each other over supper. The reality was different. The business case could well look a lot less rosy, with months of 'vacancy,' without bread on the table, numbing cold in the winter, social isolation, and so on. The image of the deranged Nicholson wandering in a daze through the corridors of his hotel in 'The Shining' came to mind without asking. Now, I always pretended not to need anyone so that social isolation would not affect me. Nicholson himself didn't fully realize how things were going downhill for him.

I fell asleep next to Ben. It is always disastrous to fall asleep for an hour and then wake up with the message that you must hurry. I am no longer really stressed about being at work on time. It was mainly the boys' school that determined my activities in the morning. Julie woke me up. The pounding headache made me wait for a hot shower and a long massage, followed by half a day between the crisp white sheets. It wasn't supposed to be. Ben and Sam were awake, and they had to hurry. When making the final choice from the new career alternatives, I would mainly be guided by the degree of freedom I could afford so that I was not tied to a pattern, a routine, or a fixed pattern. Of course, I wouldn't avoid the responsibility of my children, but if I had an 'off day' after morning obligations or just wanted to crawl into bed, that had to be possible. The black coffee brought some relief to my poor physical condition.

"Guys, hurry up. Why do I have to ask you everything ten times? Put on your coats. we're going to be late!" We might as well play that sentence on the tape recorder in the morning. How predictable. 8:10 AM, 10 minutes late, the door closed behind us after all the men had received a kiss from Julie. We got into the BMW, and off we went. The Hunters' cover version of The Smashing Pumpkins 'Bullet With Butterfly Wings,' released in 2003 on 'Low Profile,' blared through the speakers.

Even though I know - I suppose I'll show my cool and cold-like old job despite all my rage, I'm still just a rat in a cage. Despite all my rage, I'm still just a rat in a cage.

Then someone will say what is lost can never be saved despite all my rage. I'm still just a rat in a cage; now I'm naked, nothing but an animal, but can you fake it for just one more show? And what do you want? I want to change. What do you get when you feel the same?

I would go through all my options again with Fred. A fresh perspective from an outsider would do me good.

LA VIE EN ROSE

An intense buzzing in my ears as I staggered into the hotel room. Everything hurt. 4:55 AM. I automatically started zapping through the different TV channels.

My autofocus stopped working, so it took some time before I could distinguish the unashamedly licking women on the screen. My emerging erection made me suspect that this could still be inspiring. I turned off the TV, turned it over, and sprawled out on the bed. The light went out.

The plane had arrived with a delay of about 20 minutes, and since I then managed to find the luggage in Terminal A instead of Terminal B, it took an extra 40 minutes to get packed and sunk among a number of tourists in the late evening sun. Elderly, couples in love, and a few loners waiting for the bus that would transport us to the center. At this point, I had really been waiting for another month or 2. It was the fifth time I had taken this trip, and a lot had changed in that time; Ben was born, Sam was born, I became director, Julie and I had good therapy. My life was running more or less smoothly, at least that's what an outsider might think, but where I thought Marc's life was well managed, until recently anyway. Fred thought that of me. He didn't say it in so many words, but I was convinced that, in his view, I was leading a boring life. I didn't blame him because Fred was Fred, and that made him so special. The man who had always lived apart from this world seemed, the older he got, to distance himself from this earth as a kind of God and to precisely judge everything that could not be separated.

God had lived with a Spanish beauty in Barcelona for 12 years, opposite the Sagrada Familia. The day after graduating from university 'Cum Laude,' he drove to Spain with a 15-year-old Citroên Diane and his guitar. Everyone seemed to worry and make judgments about this choice. The general conclusion was that you were not wise to throw your life away like that. Fred collected money on the Rambla and continued to live in love. Of the Master(de)baters, Fred was the only one who could say that he had gone international and had actually earned money with his music.

The bus turned onto the Universitat square. We were now getting close, and the excitement of the city as I experienced it time and again took over me again. I always got a slightly 'naughty' and restless feeling about me. For me, Barcelona was the reflection of everything that 'breaking out of a straitjacket' meant. Although the apotheosis of Patrick Süskind's 'Le Parfum' took place at the Papal Palace in Avignon, there were always times when, in all my imagination, I saw the bacchanal taking place at Placa Reial, or at the cathedral, or in the alleys around San Marti. OK, this never happened in a completely fasted state, but still. My eye fell on a group of 5 ladies sitting at the back of the bus. I estimated them to be around 20. They were engaged in an animated conversation with lots of gestures and, above all, great laughter. These were probably professional bachelors who would go all out on Friday evening and party carefree until the sun came up, driving men like me crazy in the meantime. No, they would be able to drive any sane man crazy. This spectacle had carried me away for too long because the laughter had stopped, and I felt how five pairs of mostly dark female eyes had caught me. Hmmm, they would drive me crazy, but the chance of me driving them crazy was probably as good as the chance of a further glorious career within Value Creators Inc.

"Place de Catalunya," the voice called.

Grabbed my luggage and got off the bus. As soon as I got to the hotel, I called home, spoke to the 'men,' said how much I loved Julie, and then contacted Fred to inform him that I had arrived and would be visiting him on Saturday after breakfast. I was tired and didn't feel like going on a lonely restaurant expedition, and I already did enough of that for work. So I ate at the hotel and then slipped between the clean sheets around 10 PM. A few minutes later, I found myself on a dance floor in a small, heated room, with condensation and sweat running down the walls. The rhythm was pumping and killer. I felt this was going too fast for my physical constitution and coordination not to make me completely ridiculous. I got the impression that my heart rate started to adjust to the booming from the speakers, and my temples started ringing. 5 Spanish beauties danced about 2 meters in front of me, completely at one with the beat, as if their lives depended on it. And they drove me crazy.

It was already quite warm when I walked back from the Rambla towards the Place de La Catalunya around 11 o'clock on Saturday morning.

La Vie en Rose is located in C. Elisabets at number 51, on the last street on your left before you reach Place de La Catalunya. You can recognize it by the large painting on the only window of the building, above the door, which depicts Grace Jones' body as it was painted by Keith Haring in 1985 when Grace, at the height of her fame, of Island Life, performed at the Paradise Garage in NY. Fred could still wax lyrical about Grace's significance for pop music and art in general. His admiration for, and devotion to, the Jones phenomenon dated back to the early 1980s when we, as 14-15-year-old teenagers, were introduced to the city's nightlife and had our first parties. Certainly, before the heyday of the Master(de)baters, Fred was clearly the most enterprising type within our circle of friends. He was at the forefront when it came to coming up with new music, experiments in the field of soft drugs, and experience with girls and women (Fred especially managed to impress us with his experiences with older women, and the icing on the cake was perhaps that he was a tongue twisted with our Art teacher at a class party). In addition, Fred had, under his mattress, a collection of porn magazines that, if they had been under my bed, would have led to a party every night so that they would no longer have been in such a 'pure state' as when Fred's mother discovered them during cleaning on an empty stomach. While as friends, we were mainly carried away musically by the emerging New Wave (U2, Echo & the Bunnymen, The Hunters, De Simple Minds, Talk Talk. Shit, and Do you remember The Alarm) and also the 'Born in the USA' of the Boss, Fred was the man who was intensively involved with Prog Rock à la Genesis, Jazz and Grace Jones. During every listening session of our 'Burning Down,' he cannot fail to mention Grace's specific influences.

Jones' 4th CD, 'Nightclubbing' with the incredible 'Pull up to the Bumper' (baby!), became a bit of a reference point for everything that came after. Then it was also true that Grace became the icon of the Gay Scene (in a way more admirable for us than Barbara 'The Nose' Streisand.), and that made her even more special. And, of course, her appearance and Jamaican origins completed the picture of an exceptional phenomenon. Fred always dismissed every female singer who entered the charts as a second-rate Grace, whether it was Madonna, Kylie, Taylor or Dua Lipa.

My belief, however, is that Fred's real dedication came from an adventure he had at a party attended by several foreign English students. While Grace's song 'From the Nipple to the Bottom Always Satisfied' blared through the speakers, I seriously wondered why I hadn't 'Slowed Down' yet that evening, and I realized that with my attitude, I probably wouldn't. Fred climaxed on Melissa, an 18-year-old English student from Bristol. According to Fred, he wasn't the only one who had reached a climax. In fact, Melissa would have added a new dimension to the phrase 'From the Nipple to the Bottom Always Satisfied' because she had three nipples instead of 2. To this day, Fred continues to argue that this is not a myth. Whatever the case, Grace has been an integral part of Fred's life ever since.

In 1985, Grace first released the inimitable 'Slave to the Rhythm,' which, building on her popularity, was followed later that year by the compilation 'Island Life.' 'La Vie en Rose,' which had first appeared on 'Portfolio' in 1977, only now really became a hit. At the same time as the last carefree summer period and holiday that I can remember, Grace provided the musical accompaniment to the chapter that was described as 'the end of our youth' with singles such as 'La Vie en Rose' and 'Slave to the Rhythm.' And Grace was back again. After an eternity, the Hurricane album was released in 2008. A beautiful record that once again puts the Jamaican model as a respected singer in the spotlight. Songs like 'William's Blood,' 'Hurricane,' and 'Corporate Cannibal' receive a lot of airplay on radio stations and have made her announced world tour one of the most hyped events of that year.

La Vie en Rose. As soon as you walk in, you leave your current reality and enter a world of twilight, incense, and other spicy aromas and music. Record sales are 80% of what La Vie en Rose is all about, especially bootlegs on silver discs. The remaining 20% is generated by art (Fred constantly organizes exhibitions) and books, especially travel books. Fred had also entered the chill-out/lounge market for the past year. He had made a compilation album, 'La Vie en Rose I' in an edition of 100, which he gave to very good customers until he ran out of stock. A local radio station had picked up this disc and started playing songs from it. Things then moved quickly; the commercialization of the album had begun, and it was given its place in record stores next to the Buddha Bar, Paris Lounge, and Café Del Mar series. 'La Vie en Rose II' and the reissue of part I were released. The title track was again the first track on part II, and Fred stated that each series sequel would open with Grace's voice, but he wanted to try every new release to provide a different mix of the song. Since the success of these albums, Fred was regularly asked to play DJ in the places of Barcelona.

La Vie en Rose is an incredible business, and now that I looked around, I realized once again that Fred had the courage and the guts to launch something that I would dream about all my life if I didn't quickly sort out my options and would go for it. Maybe I could propose to him, as an alternative to myself, to internationalize La Vie en Rose by opening the same shop locally.

Fred had seen me come in and walked towards me from behind the counter.

"There he is, the wonderboy, the businessman. Man, you look pretty miserable."

"Thanks, dick! Good to see you again, too!"

We sank into comfortable, low armchairs at the back of the store. With Fred, it was always the case that we were immediately on the same page no matter how long we hadn't seen each other. This means that somewhere, despite our very different choices in professional and private lives, beneath the surface, we had the same feelings and shared the same opinions on many things. Fred simply had not let himself be caught by the trap that I had recently felt tighter and tighter around me, which made my armpits gush.

"That shows a fairly limited creativity," Fred responded laconically to the anecdote about the barbecue and the wish I had shouted at my colleagues in my drunken stupor.

"However, I fear that regardless of the creativity factor, the damage is just as great. Boy, I'm going off the rails so much. Now, more than ever, it is clear that I will have to make choices outside of Value Creators Inc., and perhaps John will soon urge me to take a look around. Will may not have much choice at first, but I don't think it will last. Most importantly, I've just had it, and I don't care about it anymore. The thought of Value Creators is enough to open the sweat floodgates."

"Follow your armpits! Listen to your armpits! Let your armpits do the talking!" Fred shouted.

We had a detailed discussion about the list of options I had drawn up for myself. Unlike anyone, I might have made part of these alternative future paths, but none of them was an unrealistic or idiotic choice for Fred. He did have his favorites, namely the key maker and the author. He knew my drumming abilities all too well, and that apparently didn't inspire much confidence even though he used the conservative argument of age. The Chambre D'hôte was dismissed with a "For God's sake, come up with something more original."

The hunter also deserved attention. "You could be an International Hunter who is called upon when a sick bear, wolf, or deer needs to be shot anywhere in Europe. That seems very romantic to me, but because of the traveling and the flexibility required, I recommend that you wait with that choice until you have separated from Julie." Fred loved Julie and me, yet his comment about the divorce was seriously meant because, in Fred's belief, children eventually lead to divorce. "We were created to make children, but not to have them. That is the tragedy of human existence. We are taught to reproduce, and sex is so tempting and delicious, and unfortunately, that is how children are conceived. But we don't know what to do with it. The parenting function does not exist; it was not given to us, so we muddled along. Those who succeed in managing child rearing achieve no more than a survival level; those who fail divorce, and those without children achieve happiness with little effort. Sex should actually have been a separate process that has nothing to do with fathering children. Humanity would soon be over." One of Fred's hobby horses.

"Now, I don't want to be annoying, but with your practical attitude and feeling for everything that is manual, the key maker seems a bit too far to me," Fred continued in his response to my alternatives. "I would think it is a very nice story; the successful management consultant who becomes an obscure key maker somewhere. that in itself would be a nice story for your book. Especially if you then become entangled in the worlds to which those keys would provide access. You see, that can provide you with some material for a great bestseller. Imagine what kind of film script that could entail. Man, not that you need it, but you'd be in quick. "

Looking at my clock, I realized that the morning had turned into an early afternoon. Fred had some Tapas delivered, and we switched from the Cerveza to a strong red wine. The music in the background had a heavy, chill quality, and I actually felt relaxed. It seemed like a long time ago, but I felt calm and calm for the first time in a long time.

"You have to buy this. This is Nitin Sawhney, with a song called 'Falling' from his latest album. Feels good, huh? If you really want to write a book, you can come to live with me for a few months and be inspired by the life and culture of this city. I mean by the beautiful and ugly people, the poverty and wealth, the scammers, the transvestites, the whores, and the rest of the scum of Barcelona. In fact, all the elements of a modern society, but which you breathe in and out here every day and is somehow more in your face than elsewhere. It's just an idea."

I took a large sip of wine and let it wash through all the crevices of my mouth. Shit, here I was, 38 years old, successful, father of 2 beautiful sons and a fantastic wife, talking about writing a book. Fred's offer sounded good to me but was, of course, not really worth considering; at least, I didn't want to put aside all the responsibilities I bore.

"Boy, that's a nice proposal, but it simply doesn't work. Or are you saying you would give up your apartment to the entire Jones family? Forget it. If it really comes to that, it will be after my hours. Or maybe I should make it a challenge and just write during the hours to see when they get me. God, that actually sounds like something to me?"

I enjoyed the thoughts of sitting at a desk all day, writing a book while getting paid, and, with a bit of luck, closing the Spensers deal in between. Pretty perverse.

I was pulled out of my thoughts by the Spanish words Fred spoke. I looked up and saw a pair of huge long legs in a mini skirt in front of me. I didn't really know where to look, but my pupils suddenly turned out to have a magnet that made me slide unashamedly from top to bottom over these two beautifully shaped, shiny brown legs. And despite the suppressed shame, I felt enormous relief that the magnets turned out to be in my pupils and not elsewhere.

"This is Margarita, one of my employees."

Fred introduced me to his Spanish employee, and I babbled a bit in English. Jesus, what a beautiful woman this was, probably about half my life younger; that hurt. Margarita didn't speak a word of English, and I was happy because I wouldn't have known immediately what to say (sensibly). But the hope that she would leave us alone was crushed when she settled herself on Fred's lap in her miniskirt.

"Actually, she is not a real employee (No, I actually realized that. Although Fred and I rarely talked about his private life with Marie Angeles, I had always assumed until this moment that he was fully monogamous. I actually also should know better.). She is an intern during the summer months. She is at art school here and will graduate with a degree in the meaning and impact of Grace Jones on the modeling world. She is very talented."

OK, I have to be honest. I had always admired Fred's 'independence,' the choices he made, and the ideals he pursued, but now I just felt raw jealousy. The man was the same goddamn age as me, and he was just sitting here at 1:40 PM on a Saturday afternoon with a fantastic Spanish fury of about 20 years old on his lap without looking like a forced image of a mid-thirties man, still has to if necessary and tries to convince himself that he can still do just as well with the females.

"Tonight, I will show you a tent, Gula Gula, where Maragarita's sister Eva is the owner and where we can dance against the stars again."

Perhaps because of the combination of the wine and Margarita's legs, my imagination threatened to run wild at the thought of Eva. But although Fred had said nothing about it, I knew that this would be a perhaps equally temperamental but older edition of Margarita. More specifically, Margarita's eldest sister, 29, safely and happily married, mother of 8 children, and by far the ugliest in the family. And with three brothers and four sisters, that meant something. By the way, Margarita was not actually Eva's real sister, because she was adopted when she was 3 months old.

"Eva is Margarita's twin sister. Boy, you really won't see the difference only when they dance together. Margarita is also extremely rhythmic, but Eva does have that little bit of extra sensuality, I must admit. It's always packed there on Saturday evenings, but I was able to arrange a VIP seat for us."

Margarita probably understood what it was about. She smiled emphatically in my direction, and I became acutely nervous. Just as unexpectedly as her legs had appeared, they disappeared again after she gave Fred a kiss. And although I consciously closed my eyes, I saw her shapely bottom walking away from me in the suede skirt.

I wisely suppressed my question about how Marie Angeles was doing.

I don't know how much it was, but the bottle was empty. I started to feel light-headed and let 'La Vie en Rose' sink in as Fred rolled and lit his first marijuana joint. Although Fred had smoked just about everything he could inhale, he had decided only to use marijuana this year. He had succeeded so far.

"We all get older, and whether you like it or not, our resistance decreases. Even now that I only smoke this stuff, I notice that I have to watch what I drink with it, or I will get sick. Nowadays, I limit myself to champagne, wine, whiskey, and vodka. No, not in some mixed form, but pure. Otherwise, that's the end of the story."

I had never smoked with Fred before. Not even in high school when he drank the most exotic herbs into his lungs during the break and then sat dazed on the school benches. When I smoked, I smoked at my own pace.

I took the joint and inhaled deeply.

"How is Julie?" He probably did it for that reason. I forced myself to think of Julie and the boys, watching them play in the bath together as Julie washed them and tried to keep some control over the water spectacle.

"Good, good. We're pregnant again! Not for about 3 months, but she feels good, and everything is going according to plan."

"Wait a minute! Pregnant? How long have we not emailed each other? You actually want to tell me that after Ben and Sam's quick pregnancies, Julie is now pregnant again. Boy, that's a bit of a rabbit hole. Nowadays, they have special resources for that. Contraception, or contraceptives, to be more precise. To be honest, I thought you were sufficiently of this developed world to be aware of that, and despite having two left hands, you would have figured out how to put on a condom. In a somewhat modern couple, the woman does this with a lot of love."

"Jesus, Fred, stop that nonsense. You didn't really think I was waiting for another little one, did you? But I have to be honest, and I know this definitively confirms your ideas about my bourgeoisie, the pregnancy of our third, although not expected, I experienced as something beautiful. The real misery was with Sam. I had barely recovered from the fact that Ben would stay with us for the rest of his life. Tried to get me back on track with our therapy, and BOOM, it was a hit! Man, you should know the shock when I found out Julie was pregnant. I cursed and really felt bad about it. Have you ever seen 'She is having a baby'? The moment that guy is informed by his wife. Remember that, with that locomotive crashing really hard against a wall. Fuck boy, but that was the feeling I had. The bad thing was that I was just in London closing a big deal when I got a phone call. Julie was in tears, and I couldn't hear anything, just crying. I really thought there had been deaths. And when I really understood what was really going on, I had the feeling that people had actually died. Julie was actually crying with joy, but because she was afraid of my reaction, it was the fear she was expressing. The absurd thing is that I quickly felt proud that I had managed to do it again. Wow, you don't actually want to be as fertile as I am. And while I was stimulated in my male euphoria, and of course, I felt nice and 'Sharp' about it, I slowly but surely realized that this would, of course, become another product with a long shelf life.

The strange thing is actually, and now it's probably getting really creepy for you, that I have to admit that I now feel happy with the arrival of the third one. Really. I see you turning pale, but I mean it. Now, for the first time, I have the feeling that 'we' are pregnant."

Fred looked at me in disbelief.

"I agree with you that having children is never an emotional choice for men. Suppose they make that choice consciously and do not allow themselves to be seduced by a weak moment of too much alcohol, an intensive, well-executed massage, or beautiful black lingerie. Is it rational based on the belief that this will make their wife happier, but without any understanding of the consequences? Men lack that primal feeling of creating and carrying life. It's that old story of the hunter, after all. Anyway, believe it or not, I'm a happy man.. or is that because of that Marijuana?" I joked and took another deep drag on the joint, closed my eyes, and let the inhaled smoke create a haze of darkness in my head.

"I know your theory about sex and children. Well, in fact, here in front of you is living proof of your statement. Uncomplicated sex? Forget it. Behind every temptation, tantra massage, or Kama Sutra position lies the image of a screaming baby, and yet we allow ourselves to be seduced. However, you forget that as a man, once the children are there, you really experience the difference and see and feel the 'added value' of those little people. Fuck, it really is a miracle."

Fred shook his head.

"The difference between man and woman is fantastic. For the man, impregnating the woman is actually nothing more and nothing less than influencing a 'hit rate.' In your case, that was already a glorious hat trick; they won't take that away from you anymore. I think the man is only doing that 'hit rate,' and absolutely not because he is deliberately trying to fulfill his desire to have children. I don't believe in a rational choice either; a man is too selfish for that. A birth or miscarriage ultimately makes no difference to the man. For women, it is completely different. The urge to nest, the motherly feeling, you know it. That means that at a certain moment, the woman really longs for a little one, usually at the moment when the sparks within the relationship are finally extinguished and so-called real love enters. That always sets off alarm bells for me, but that's beside the point. So, the woman, also stimulated by the biological clock, gets a firm grip and wants to become pregnant and ultimately give birth. You understand that I am actually extremely frustrated because my hit rate is zero for the time being. Fortunately, for men like me, there are other elements that can stroke the ego. That is the story of a completely different hit rate."

I listened attentively, but at the moment, I couldn't quite decide whether these were wise words or complete nonsense.

I felt empty in the head but did not have the impression that I was heavily under the influence of marijuana. I actually didn't really know what effect I should expect. The clarity of mind and calmness about me certainly made me happy.

"You know what? We're going to get away from this. I'm taking you to a special place. For me, it is a bit like the covered Placa Reial. I usually play there on Friday evenings. I suggest we eat there. Maybe I'll meet some acquaintances there who can help improve the atmosphere at Eva later."

Half an hour later, we entered the alleys around Marché de Santa Caterina and walked through the C. De la Princesa via the C. Montcada past the Picasso Museum to the C. Ribera, next to the Marché del Born. It was now 7:30 PM and still early by Spanish standards. But the good thing about Born-Neo was that you could go there from 6:00 PM until 3:00 AM.

"Most people work here until about 8 or 9 in the evening, and you won't find them here during the week, but the real people who don't care much about traditional working patterns can come here when they want to. You will see that there are quite a lot of artists and artistic figures and a lot of beautiful people. The modeling world of Barcelona has also recently discovered this place. Especially, of course, following the publication of 'La Vie en Rose II' and the fact that I came to perform here in person on Friday. You will see that you are short of eyes. We can also enjoy very good Basque dishes there.

Boy, cheer up, tonight you will be "Corrected." Tonight, you will once again feel alive; I guarantee you that! Tonight, you will find out again in some way that you are in trouble."

Messing around in my body ?!

My thoughts spontaneously went out to Margarita, Eva, and Julie!

Like a huge bolt of lightning, my wife arrived in my upstairs room. Dammit, I should have called a long time ago.

"I don't care what you're going to do there, and like every year, I don't want to know," she said before I left. "I don't really need to hear you, although I would, of course, enjoy that, but you make sure you have spoken to the men before they get into bed. You know they love that."

Almost 8 PM, one day away from home, I had completely forgotten my obligations (which were very limited, let's be honest.). No, of course, that was not due to bad intentions, but perhaps to the Marijuana in combination with that little bit of drink, but explain that.

"Hey Sam, man, how's the boyfriend? Did you have a nice bath? What..no, tell mommy daddy isn't drunk. NOT DRUNK! Dad just spent a lot of time on Marijuana this afternoon. No, not Hakuna Matata, but Marihuana. And now it's a bit dark in Dad's head, and Dad kind of forgets that he's Ben and Sam's dad, so Dad forgot to call you on time. But daddy loves you. You know that, don't you, boy?"

Jesus, what an embarrassing display.

"Shit, Fred, I have to make an urgent call to reassure the home front and to wish the boys good night."

I called the number as we arrived at the entrance to Born-Neo. It was a huge building with an entrance through a small wooden door in a huge green gate. The building appeared to be an old factory building from the 1920s. Fred spoke Spanish, shook hands, and we were let in. We crossed a courtyard, walked up two floors via a steel staircase on the outside of the building, and suddenly stood on an inside balcony looking out over a beautiful room, dimly lit by a red glow, black marble on the floor, and azure blue mosaic stones all over the wall. A color combination that looked horrible on paper but was breathtaking in reality.

"Hello." the child psychiatrist's voice sounded familiar. Familiar short. I had lost all my points, and it sounded like if I finally called now, I could only lose more. I didn't really know what to say, and I also suspected that every statement would come across as ridiculous despite my deep sense of guilt. The good intentions and the sentimentality that came over me. The latter, in particular, was always received with suspicion and dismissed with a "You must have had too much to drink again." Tonight was no different. I briefly considered starting the discussion and elaborating on the enriching feeling that Marijuana can give you, but I let the thoughts be nipped in the bud by

Julie's deep, reproachful sigh and perhaps the disconnect that followed.

I put my cell phone away and looked into the room where Fred had found a table. There were also two women and a man at the table. As I entered the room and approached the table, thoughts of home faded. I concentrated and tried to hold on to my guilt, but when I got to the table, the only thing that touched me was the look in Anna's eyes, which were looking intently at me as I shook her hand. The scent I smelled when I kissed her on the neck made me dizzy. She was introduced by Fred at the same time as the tall blonde, shapely Garcia and Aitor, the man in the group. What their relationship with Fred was completely escaped me, so strongly was I drawn to Anna. She was a woman who reminded me enormously of the successful tennis player of the 80s, the Argentinian Gabriela Sabatini, who had caused many a wet dream, including a specific 'Action Shot,' Sabatini serving with her skirt up her leg crawls, and the nipple of her right breast pierces right through the tight, sweat-soaked T-shirt, is burned into my retina. Anna had the same broad shoulders and those heavy cheekbones. I guessed she was about 6 feet tall and probably in her early 30s. She was dressed in a tight black dress with a huge cleavage that just didn't end. At least, I didn't dare look any further. She wore black stiletto heels. Her smile was radiant, and she had a row of fantastically beautiful teeth. Her black hair shone and hung down over her broad shoulders.

My God, what a woman. Fred looked at me with a grin. I had a glass of champagne and toasted it with the whole group. With the first sip, I closed my eyes and tried to remember my most important appointments for next week. I couldn't do it. I downed the remaining contents of the glass and was overcome by the husky voice of Anna speaking to me in fluent English.

"So you're Fred's best friend. You must be quite someone, then. How do you know each other?"

I felt a bit shy and searched for words. Opted for the dry factual explanation.

"We ended up sitting next to each other in the 2nd year of high school. I think that at first, we didn't really like each other and turned a bit of a blind eye, but over time, we noticed that we were on the same wave spring." My thoughts went back to my years in high school and then our time together in college. We followed completely different directions, Fred in communication sciences and myself in business economics, but we met every week to discuss the meaning of life and the most important priorities you had to set within it. Every Thursday, we had a drinking session during which a few world problems were solved, and then, relieved after work was done, we threw ourselves into the nightlife. Either one of them ended up drunk on the other's hard wooden floor, spending the night only under a raincoat or a lead coat (and guaranteed to wake up with a huge hangover), or one of them (Fred is far from most cases) to hook a woman to let off some steam from the accumulated hormonal tensions. Memorable opinions and solutions? Legion.

Which direction to wipe your butt after a hard session? That discussion didn't last long. There were, in fact, only two options (swiping to the sides was not realistic, in our opinion, and we did not want to spend our valuable time on purely theoretical analyses.): either you swiped up, or you swiped down. Assuming that we were fully heterosexual, which was an important sine qua non, it seemed obvious to us that swiping up towards the back was better than swiping down. After all, the idea that you ran the risk of spreading odor towards your scrotum was too much.

What was the most ridiculous invention? We didn't go out there in one evening. After the necessary intensive sessions and bottles of cheap wine resulting in the necessary expenses, it was decided that creating 'pets' (with the dog in the lead) was the most idiotic invention of man. This meant that the moped (a machine that, even fully tuned up, could not sufficiently control the testosterone of the 16-year-old boy while making an enormously irritating noise), Sinterklaas (a commercial phenomenon consciously created by a society that allowed children to experience trauma with impunity). by having the Spanish bishop exposed as Uncle David, the neighbor or another acquaintance, and which gave parents all the means to compensate for their pedagogical shortcomings), and the coffin with the associated funeral (We did not understand why people between 6 planks were pushed a meter under the turf when they had left earthly life). Was it out of fear that they might not turn out to be dead and that they were in danger of coming back to life and thus disrupting the grieving processes and expectations of those left behind? Or from a habit originated by loved ones who did not know what to do with the dead person, and where life announced itself naturally and automatically through the revelation of a belly, there was no natural 'back door' through which the dead person entered the nothing could solve) to lose out.

Who was the most important musical person of our time? Ok, we couldn't figure it out straight away. Head and shoulders Grace Jones if it were up to Fred.

"It also turned out that we had a bit of the same sense of humor," I said. "But that was usually not the same as that of the teachers. However, Fred generally knew damn well how far he could go to avoid taking any risks. On the other hand, I usually understood where I should have drawn the line if I was expelled or suspended again, completely wrongly, of course. Don't think that had to do with being a coward or anything. He was just smarter."

"Well, at least it didn't drive you two apart."

Anna handed me a new glass of champagne. The space started to fill up with a lot of hip people of very different ages and backgrounds. The women were generally young. I estimated the average to be 25 years old. This was clearly the place to be. The spectacle of lights created constantly changing atmospheres. Anna and I suddenly stood in a very intimate pink twilight light. The volume of the music had increased. A series of samples, dry beats, and thin voices created the optimal lounge ambiance.

"So, what beautiful and challenging things do you deal with in your daily life?"

Her right leg slid down my right knee. The suspender was exposed.

"Uuuh, challenging?"

The champagne filled my mouth and washed away the lump in my dry throat. Still, nothing came. Because I didn't dare to move and stood stiffly, I realized that we must look idiotic, especially since Anna made no move to pull her leg away or rearrange her dress. I stood slightly apart, slightly bent at the knees. Suddenly, it reminded me of my first ski lesson, where, in the same position, I noticed that I was going faster and faster without having any control over the direction or speed. It was getting harder and harder today, and my grip on the direction seemed just as uncertain. I wondered if I had adopted this attitude for a long time.

Now, it also turned out that I was holding my empty champagne glass in front of me with both hands. Rather, the phenomenon of the ski lift. I had to take action quickly.

I took a breath and opened my mouth But, still, nothing came. Anna winked and happily broke the silence.

"Dance?"

My God, that too. We shifted back and forth to a sultry, fat, slow bass thump. This was seriously going wrong here. Fred, Fred, Where's Fred? Screamed in my head as Anna's tongue made circular movements near my earlobe. My right hand was apparently disconnected from the cry for help in my head, and I actively searched for Anna's right buttock. The thumb settled on the seam of her thong and began to make a sort of 'leapfrog' motion.

An olive found easy access to my mouth. A willing tongue was at his heels, straining to overtake the olive.

"You can't do this!"

Fred! My savior. I could always count on him.

"If you really want to let yourself go and I have to turn a blind eye, then damnit not with a transsexual." "You Tarzan," she said, "Not a second time, buddy."

Like a pinball machine, the olive first shot into the back of my throat and then was fired in the opposite direction like a bullet. "Jackpot!" I gasped. Anna winked again, turned, and walked away.

"It's been nice here; let's go to better places where you are not in danger of risking your pure heterosexuality. Or is it psychologically easier for you to accept cheating with anything but a real woman? However, I don't think it will matter to Julie."

Outside, I inhaled the warm air with deep breaths. It was a sultry summer evening, and the sky was full of stars.

"So you knew about her, or should I say her., past, and you just framed me. You are a nice friend!"

"Boy, don't you turn on so much? You have to admit that if all the women in this world looked like this, it would be a more pleasant place. I mean, the operations went well. And, after all, it's the personality that matters. Forget what happened and focus on what is to come. But, I warn you, I won't save you a second time!"

We remained silent and walked for what felt like several kilometers through small streets and narrow alleys. It was now 10:15 PM. The evening was still young, and I felt terribly old. The previous times with Fred had been calm and inspiring simply because of the long conversations we had and the confirmations or insights that the discussions provided. Last year was the first time I visited Fred in La Vie en Rose. He had had the business for almost one year. After a long period of playing the guitar and living on expenses and the goodwill of the woman, Fred had responded to an advertisement asking for a 'setter' for a Record store. Due to his broad musical interests and knowledge, the idea of showcasing Grace Jones, and the original name for the business, he was immediately hired. It did not provide a fat salary, but it did provide a pleasant job and a lot of freedom. By launching 'La Vie en Rose I' and the publicity that entailed, Fred managed to grow from an anonymous foreign tourist into an eccentric belonging to Barcelona's in-crowd. With the release of the second album, the name recognition of the store and its 'owner' took on extraordinary proportions. Fred became a man in demand and also started to create fame as a DJ. Things can go pretty damn fast. One year, you are still living on the margins (but happy), and the next moment, you are a celebrated VIP in the prime of your life. Perhaps I should take courage and hope from that.

The big difference with Fred, however, was that he did not attach importance to material possessions, that, of course, he had no responsibilities as I did (as I thought about it, I tried with all my might not to remember the names and images of Julie, Ben, and Sam.) and that he was already happy before he changed his life. But still, who knows where I would be in a year's time.

"Look, it can be done here."

We had walked into a dead-end hallway. At the end was a dark, heavy metal door that reminded me of the locked entrance to an electricity shed.

"This is it. How do we get in here?"

"You can only come in here if you have the correct mobile number, so we have to dial that now. That number is changed every time and only passed on to the 'Invitees.' It is a fairly small club and can accommodate a maximum of 300 people. I was lucky enough to get to know Margarita. Otherwise, I wouldn't have been able to introduce you here, but for me, it is the absolute number one in terms of nightlife in Barca. Hopefully, expectations are not too high."

Fred dialed a number and spoke some Spanish words, and we waited for the door to open. I was very curious and longed for the drink.

Through the door, we entered a hall lit only by enormous drip candles that were placed on the wall about 3 meters high. There was no music to be heard and nothing special to see. The corridor slowly widened, and through a kind of funnel shape, we suddenly found ourselves in an arena. I can't call it anything else. It was a round room with darkened vaults on the sides and low seats and tables. The arena itself was empty. In the center, I observed an enormous pole that seemed endlessly long, disappearing into the pupil of a huge lifelike eye at the narrowest, highest part of the circular ceiling. A round balcony was attached halfway up the pole. Here, too, the lighting was mainly created by enormous candles mounted at different levels on the terra cotta wall. Furthermore, horizontal spotlights with muted yellow light, placed sporadically on the ground, created special effects with long shadows on the wall.

"Great club, huh? And look at what beautiful people are. Just take a good look around. I'm going to get some tapas and drinks. What do you want?"

"If they have some good red wine here, I'll give it a try." Fred disappeared, and I let my eyes scan the room. While I was mainly trying to spot people in the dark vaults, as I was the only one standing in plain sight at the edge of the arena, I saw a silhouette moving from the other side, moving through the center of the arena towards me. I squinted a little to better see what the person looked like. Abruptly, a girl stepped out of the shadows.

"Hola!" Margarita's smiling face looked at me.

"Hola you too," I stammered. She beckoned to me, and I followed her through the arena, looking around to make sure I didn't see Fred. The music I heard was of an extremely New Age quality, with smooth violins, twittering birds, and swirling water. Completely meaningless wallpaper music. Fred had previously announced that the dance numbers would be played from about 11 o'clock, and then I would experience something else. Margarita took me to a secluded salon where Fred had apparently settled down. There was also Giuseppe, a young man in his 40s, I guessed, who spent his life as a nature photographer; Andrew, a 38-year-old gay British man who had lived in Spain for 20 years and ran a chain of hair salons in the city; François, a Parisian who spent 6 months a year portraying 'Still Lifes' on the Rambla to finance his travels for the remaining 6 months; Marie José, a dynamic, charming, although not particularly beautiful, young woman who made jewelry and sold it through her own shop and recently also through La Vie en Rose; and finally Louise, a Canadian shapely young woman who has been making a living as a dancer in Barcelona for three years. Tonight, she would dance here. It was a colorful and mixed group that made my 'Civilian' life a bit sad. At least, that's what I felt. I exchanged a few words with everyone. They were very friendly and seemed interested in my friendship with Fred and what I did professionally. I got into a deeper conversation with Louise, probably because the language barrier is lower, I thought as I tried to keep my eyes off her beautiful body that was dressed in a revealing dance outfit. Louise had straw-blond hair, done up casually with a few strands and strands falling along her face. She had almost black eyes and heavy eyebrows, a beautiful nose with beautiful nostrils, and a full mouth.

"So you are Fred's infamous, yet hidden and therefore mysterious, best friend. How do you two actually know each other?"

For a moment, this opening question made me suspicious, and I tried to find out whether this lady might have a past like Louis's, but she made an authentic impression. In addition, I didn't expect to be the victim of sexual harassment for the second time that evening, so I felt quite comfortable.

Louise was 28 years old and had studied chemistry (Chemistry?. Chemistry! This had to be a joke), then started working as an assistant at the University of Vancouver and, after about 5 years and almost finished her PhD, she could use the money she had earned to make a long journey that would drastically change her life. She traveled alone, with only a backpack, from Canada to Asia to discover Cambodia, Vietnam, Thailand, and South India. I tried to imagine how this woman traveled through Asia alone and unscathed. I really wondered why people traveled alone in the first place and how it was possible that such a beautiful woman did not have a whole horde of potential travel companions to travel around in the first place and then managed to travel alone during the trip.

"You're going a little too fast. First of all, you travel alone. Even if you think you have to do that with others, it is such a personal experience in what you observe, smell, absorb, and feel and the intensity with which you experience it all in your contact with others who have traveled the same journey and the same something like this is only frustrating because it painfully exposes how individualistic we are while the pressure to be social, to 'Share' and to be on the same wavelength is so great. I met a guru in Mahalabaripuram, Swali Pakrash, with whom I had an exceptional experience."

'Guru' flashed through my mind. I had overlooked that as a potential option. It shouldn't be really difficult to settle somewhere, adhere to a vague philosophy, and then communicate it to men or, preferably, women in a smart way. If I wanted to appear a bit serious, I, of course, had to change my name instead of Sai Baba or Swali Pakrash, something like Heroin Harry. Now that I have taken a good look at Louise, I have come to the conclusion that it did not have to be just 'lost cases' who were tempted into a session with the Guru. An 'Exceptional Experience' The only thing I could imagine was Louise panting and puffing, gushing with sweat, through an impossible position (only to appear in Kama Sutra, the sequel) to a mega orgasm by her Guru. Hmmmm, maybe I should reconsider my options.

I listened attentively.

"He made me realize that I was living a life that was not my own. I did everything to meet the expectations of those around me, and I did nothing on my own because I wanted to. And so I lived a life without passion. He told me to do something with my body."

Jesus Christ, I thought, could it be any more banal? "He told her to do something with her body." What a brilliantly earth-shattering and enlightening idea.

Louise continued undisturbed. "I then took an Indian dance course in the ashram where I was, which gave me the feeling that I was coming home. Really, I didn't know what was happening I had never known such an intense feeling of happiness. That made me realize that I had to give up everything, throw off my straitjacket, and become a dancer. So, after my tour through Asia, I traveled to Europe, visiting Italy, Portugal, and Spain, and in Barcelona, I was lucky enough to be able to dance in a number of clubs. And voilà, it's happening here tonight. I enjoy every minute."

So that was her story: from almost a chemistry doctor to a club dancer in a nutshell. That wasn't much stranger than from a successful management consultant to a key maker or author. Louise turned to me again.

"But to get back to your comment. You assume that I didn't meet any interesting people along the way and spent parts of my journey with them. Of course, but those were chance encounters that were part of the adventure nothing was planned, and those travel contacts always only lasted a short time.

Yes, I see you looking in a way that confirms what you insinuated in your question, namely that you think that my possible traveling companions are always also my sex partners."

I had to regroup for a moment. I almost regretted speaking to her because Louise's words were quite strong, and I couldn't deny that, as she talked about her journey, I wondered how many horny travelers and 'would-be' adventurers had slept with this woman next to the Swali. She noticed me and confronted me with it in a gentle manner. I took a long sip of my red wine to steady myself before simply admitting that she was on to me when she handed me a whopper of a joint.

"That's it for tonight's more substantive confrontational conversations," I thought as I took a deep breath in relief.

"You don't seem like the type to smoke marijuana or take other drugs, but you look like it could do you some good. You don't have to give me an explanation. But be a little careful, especially if you drink too much alcohol."

I let the comment sink in, along with the wine and the joint. I now had to allow myself to be seduced into a painfully profound conversation with a complete stranger. A conversation in which I would openly discuss my doubts and options, which for a lady like Louise would certainly lead to the obvious conclusion that I had ended up in a serious, typical midlife crisis. In that case, would I run the risk of ending up crying on this beautiful woman's shoulder under the influence of the drink, the drugs, and my general state? That would be terribly embarrassing, and it would also deprive me of the opportunity to benefit from the dancing twins, Margarita and Eva, I thought as Molokko's 'Forever More' blasted through the speakers, as an announcement of the dance festival that was now taking place had really begun.

But what is the difference between these individuals who do the things they like and those who, like Louise, were initially on the wrong track.? Why should something like this be age-related at all, I thought as I inhaled again sharply. While I followed the smoke rings that I blew upwards, I observed a blinded black dancer on the balcony halfway up the pole, where she accompanied the rhythm in tiny white briefs and a bra like a contortionist. Ok, I was 38 and had made some choices in my life that I couldn't simply deny or ignore, but who had the right to dismiss the doubt and rethinking options as a mid-life crisis? And the fact that I was involved in music, buying the Q, the Uncut, and sometimes the Arena every month, was not in itself a shame, was it? On the other hand, when I spoke to John, and he listed to me the articles from the FT, The Economist, and the Harvard Business Review that he had read over a weekend, I always automatically had a self-reproachful reflex of 'grow up'. and I usually nodded in agreement. Of course, I didn't dare mention the record fair I visited over the weekend in search of an obscure bootleg of a REM concert dating back to 1991 when they performed under the name Bingo Hand Job at the Shocking Club in Milan. Shit, but regardless of age and the etiquette that society places on you when you make drastic choices 'At Age,' the only thing that matters is that you are happy! I felt a sudden euphoria come over me as if I could take on the world I want to hold on to this feeling, I thought, once again pulling on my joint with my eyes closed.

Hmmmmm, it was about time I met Eva.

The moment I made eye contact with Andrew, I saw that he started walking in my direction, and I realized that the language barrier was, unfortunately, just as low with him as with Louise; Fred was suddenly next to me.

"How are you? Do you like it a bit? I've already told you, but if you want to write a book you should come and live in Barcelona for a while. You meet so many different interesting people here and gain so much inspiration that your novel will flow naturally from the pen. Louise is also an interesting woman, no? What do you think of my friends?"

"An interesting company and a group of people who all give me the impression that they are passionate about their work. That sounds pretty soft, but I think they are a happy bunch. I think it's because they all make something I mean really creating something. Andrew cuts away, François creates his own world based on his photos, and Louise designs a new view of the world every evening based on her body and dance. You've already put together two damn albums, and you're spinning the globe, so to speak, any way you want when you put together one exotic record after another. I think it's time for a radical change this year and that I should start doing my own thing instead of selling a vague product to a customer for a lot of money based on so-called best practices and a good bullshit story without any added value. Value: A combination of euphoria and wantonness took over me. A warm glow and a bizarre feeling of excitement overcame my body. Yes, I would recommend them to Value Creators Inc. I wanted to blow my mind by taking some drastic measures that would once and for all turn my future in a positive direction.

"Kylie Minogue is especially good at creating a sultry, horny atmosphere. And may I just point out that this lady is the same age as me," I said with a glassy look in my eyes and a big smile on his face when he recognized the beat of 'Can't Get You out of My Head.'

"I don't know about you, but I think we should show them here again how we can let loose to good music. And with all those beautiful women people around, the inspiration will be great. Let me first introduce you to Eva so that you can distinguish between Margarita and Eva when the 'Spanish Twins' let themselves go. I think she's still in the locker room right now. Come on."

We moved through the dancing crowd to a dimly lit room located between the toilets. In the dressing room, a small room of about 9 m², the sparse bluish lighting was enhanced by a mirror that extended over all the walls. A few spotlights had been installed on the left wall to provide additional lighting for the dressing table, where two ladies were getting ready. Upon entering, one of the ladies turned towards us while the other continued to look undisturbed in the mirror, and her bare breasts swayed with the movements her hands made to apply mascara to the long eyelashes carefully. My gaze completely ignored the first lady. I immediately recognized Eva by her face and eyes, which resembled Margarita's like two peas in a pod. Now, I also got a few pearls of breasts in the bargain, which, for the time being, only gave me a dry mouth. After listening to Fred's greeting, Eva wiped her eyes, stood up without any embarrassment, and came to kiss him. The first lady, a certain Inez, I was later told by Fred, had introduced herself and left without me noticing. Unlike Margarita, Eva turned out to speak English very well.

"Hi, Fred. Glad to see you. You should have come earlier. I have to get up in 5 minutes and then you know I'll be busy for the rest of the evening. Would you like to speak and get to know you, Harry. I've heard a lot from you, but you'll have to wait until very late because I still have to deal with the last customers and the closing after dancing. But stay as long as you want, and I expect you on the dance floor."

I stood transfixed, listening to this stunning woman with equally beautiful breasts whose nipples stared at me from all corners of the room in a way that made me shy and blush.

"We're going to have a good time, and maybe we'll talk to you and Margarita later. The evening is still young! Do your best because I promised Harry that you are the best dancers in Barcelona."

"Ciao," Eva said as she kissed me on my cheek, whispering, "Hope to see you later" in my ear. On her shoulder, I noticed a beautiful blue butterfly tattooed with great craftsmanship.

"Hope to see you later?" I must have come up with that myself If she did say that, it would probably be her standard line for every man she kissed. And there would inevitably be a lot of them.

We left the dressing room to return to the arena, which had now turned into a swirling, dancing sea. The temperature in the dance temple and the volume of the music had risen considerably. Fred and

I were about the only ones standing at the side of the dance floor, drinking another glass of champagne. It was half past twelve, Saturday evening in the Gula Gula, and I was about to 'throw myself.' This could be a beautiful evening. I tried to summon Eva's breasts, but due to an acute short circuit, I received an angry look from Julie instead. Drinking my glass in one gulp with my eyes closed did not help. In fact, Julie's eyes were now literally breathing fire. I turned decisively and made my way through the dancing crowd to the center of the arena to the beat of Madonna's 'Hollywood.' Julie's eyes burned into my back. Shit, I had to lose her. I kept pushing forward through the crowd of violently dancing and moving characters until I was sure Julie had lost herself. I closed my eyes and let myself go. This bird has flown.

The next few hours were spent dancing intensely and letting the music take me away from the effects of the previous day's booze and marijuana. I loved dancing because it gave me a feeling of absolute freedom, especially to my favorite songs. Tonight, as if in ecstasy, I reached a level of 'looseness' that I had never experienced before. My body also seemed to get into a cadence that could easily handle every beat. Sweat ran down from my temples and forehead while my T-shirt and even my pants were soaked. Despite the limited space that I had to share with about 300 swinging people, I was completely introverted, fully enjoying the moment and the happiness I experienced.

It was Grace's 'Pull up to the Bumper' that opened my eyes. I took in the heaving crowd of people surrounding me. I was once again struck by how many beautiful and beautifully moving women had gathered in just a few square meters.

I vaguely remembered a situation with five young dancing ladies but couldn't understand the exact reason and location.

My eye fell on Fred, who was experiencing a sensual couple dance with Margarita and Eva. Along with the sweat, sex dripped from their bodies as they passed a huge joint to each other. Although Eva's breasts were now hidden under a tense silk turquoise band, my senses were stimulated even more than in the dressing room. I had to swallow the excess saliva in my mouth. Eva had seen me, broke away from Fred, and moved towards me. In full consciousness, I grabbed her and then became one with her in a dance that was new to me. We didn't exchange words and consciously sought each other's eyes. There was no embarrassment or avoidance, just the active will to challenge and experience this moment together. She passed me the joint, which I accepted with great enthusiasm, pulling on it with my eyes closed. Apparently, today's entire dose of drink and drugs had decided to launch an unexpected frontal attack. The speed at which my head started spinning took me by surprise. I grabbed around desperately because even with my eyes open, I kept spinning around. Fortunately, the pole was within reach. Margarita's body came to complete rest as if in slow motion. She was soaking wet; strands of hair hung drenched along and over her face while her beautiful body shone. Big, dark eyes stared at me.

No matter how hard I tried, I couldn't capture the words that came to me. My eye fell on the butterfly that flew away from her shoulder and circled up the pole towards the pupil in the ceiling. I spread my wings and burst free from the heaving crowd. Below me, among the dancing audience, who were swaying as if on a wave to the sounds of 'Rhythm is a dancer' by Snap, I saw an older young person, moving somewhat uncomfortably, surrounded by a number of women, which drove him wild. The more women started to undress, the more butterflies flew around my head. Purple, green, azure blue, and all kinds of colors fluttered before my eyes, and I tried to get away by changing direction with quick, short strokes. I saw the wall too late and tried to avoid the dripping candle. They had looked like small candles from the bottom, but now I could no longer avoid the one-and-a-half-meter one. The blow was enormous.

I spent the time from about four in the morning until Fred greeted me in the lobby, spinning around in the bathroom like a dog trying to catch its own tail. This recurring rotation was inspired by the peristaltic movements that followed each other faster and faster and that, at the very last moment, moved in the direction of the mouth or the anus. Fortunately, I kept hitting the enamel of the toilet bowl neatly again and again. Over time, both of my exit channels burned so badly that I was tempted to verify whether there was actually no fire involved. By 9 AM, I was drained and physically broken. My head was about to burst. The half-hour I spent sitting in the shower tray, with the spray aimed straight at the top of my head, also yielded little results. Finally, I got into my clothes and went down to the lobby, where I had arranged to meet Fred for breakfast before heading to the airport.

"The Shroud of Turin is among us," Fred said with a broad grin.

I wisely skipped breakfast and only had black coffee. Fred and I slowly and at length discussed the experiences of the previous day. He thought I had behaved very nicely. Everything he said made me try to remember what exactly had happened. I was not really derailed, but when going over yesterday's events, I had the impression that, on the one hand, they were anecdotes that only someone else could have experienced, and on the other hand, if it had not been a pure dream for myself, it certainly implied that I was losing the pedals. That's damn typical; when you're already with a huge hangover, you also get a depressing, hopeless thought.

The plane took off at 12:40 and brought me back to everyday reality in about 2 hours. I wondered how much of that reality would still be mine.

TOP 5

On Monday at 8 AM, I entered my office. The weekend was hard for me. On Saturday afternoon, Julie and the boys met me when I got home. Already on the plane, I started to look forward to seeing them again. I also felt good about Julie; after all, I had managed to hold my own despite all the temptations. I would tell her the story of my day with Fred, including the contacts I had made with Margarita, Anna, Louise, and Eva. I would proudly tell you how these ladies had started talking to me and made advances, and I had gloriously managed to resist the temptation. Hell, I hadn't even watched the porn channel in my hotel room.

From the moment I put the key in the door, Ben and Sam were crazy. Julie responded less enthusiastically. A cold kiss on the cheek was all that could be done. I spent the afternoon mainly playing with the children, so the icy atmosphere between Julie and I remained in the air until 8 PM, when the two boys were in bed. The evening with Julie had ended badly. Once again, I felt a constant mistrust of superficial talk about the children, and my stay in Barcelona was not covered up or removed.

I had taken extra strong coffee, also because I had the impression that there were still some herbs in my blood, which meant that my whole being was still not completely back on earth, and I tried not to think about the previous evening when my mobile phone rang, and John's number appeared. Jesus, let me rest, I thought...

John would normally, pre-barbecue, inquire about my stay in Barcelona, post a few comments about Spanish beauties, and then quickly switch to the e-HR deal with Spensers. His small talk would now be kept to a minimum post-barbecue; after all, we were no longer really on speaking terms.

No way I'm letting the week start so badly.

"Hey Harry, did you have a good weekend in Barca? Beautiful city, isn't it? Good restaurants and hot chicks. When you lie on the beach and look around, you spontaneously turn onto your stomach... Ha, ha, ha." He held the mobile phone half a meter from my ear and downed another sip of strong coffee. John, still friendliness itself... Could that guy have a library of standard templates on his mobile phone that he could play depending on the person he was calling? Maybe it was because of John's comment about hot women, but suddenly Eva's breasts spontaneously popped into view, pushing John's arrogant face away from my retina.

"Um, what are you saying...? Spensers? Uuuh, Spensers." The breasts rushed out of the picture under light pressure and made way for Eric Spensers, current CEO of Spensers. Following the management meeting 2 months ago, and especially after the disastrous event at Will's home, I only had one goal, or assignment, because I did not experience it as a goal, to work out and close the deal with Spensers. 'Close.' I had tried a few times to have serious discussions with Eric, but it apparently cost him as much effort as it did me. I had gotten to the point where, in my view, the CEO must find it very entertaining, if not less, and had made a hobby of keeping consultants busy and holding out carrots, knowing there would never be a deal. The week after the barbecue and the good Monday morning conversation with Will, I flew with Erik Spensers to our Shared Services Center in Budapest. Eric had already consumed 3 small bottles of Veuve Clicquot on the plane, and the tone was set with a few insinuations about his honorary membership of the 10,000 miles club. Eric was received with all due respect in Budapest. He received a beautiful leather folder with the logo of our Shared Services Center and a 24-carat Cross pen pushed into the holder. "I like this. That's what I want...." he beamed like a child when I presented him with the folder. Then, the presentation began, which would be followed by a tour. However, an hour into the presentation, Eric had to leave urgently to make unforeseen crisis conference calls...

I felt quite embarrassed because the Value Creators Inc. team had spent a lot of time on this day. Anyway, it was about a potentially important customer. After lunch with the Value Creators Inc. team, I received a telephone call from Spensers' secretary informing me that Eric would no longer be able to attend meetings.

The 'no longer being able to do it' took on a very specific meaning for me when, after lunch at the Vaci Utca, I saw Eric Spensers staggering out of a brasserie with a blonde lady in a fur coat on both arms. My imagination may have gone completely crazy, but on closer inspection, I thought I recognized the two women from the article I had read on the plane about the endlessly growing and increasingly perverse porn industry in the former Eastern Bloc, with Budapest as the cradle... The article was embellished with a number of photos of actresses stating their track record in the business. Deciding not to confront Eric about my presence, I returned to the hotel and emailed John a brief report of our stay that afternoon. I was aware that I should not let my cynicism prevail, and within Value Creators, I had also learned how to create my own reality and reassure myself and John with a far-reaching form of 'self-fulfilling prophecy.' So I leaned over my laptop and typed:

Hey John,

Constructive meeting here in the Shared service center. I have now gotten to know Eric more personally, and that is a good thing. Of course, the poker face doesn't always show it, but I think he is very impressed with our capability. At one point, he even said, 'I like this; that's what I want.' So a good investment, I think.

Hopefully, upon our return, we can make a follow-up appointment together shortly and further shape the deal in concrete terms. Keep you informed.

Cheers,

Harry

That follow-up appointment did not happen. In fact, Eric had missed his plane, and I had made no further attempt to follow up.

"Yes, when will we finally have that agreement to reach concrete agreements? It's already been more than 2 weeks since you were in Hungary. You have to be quick on the ball, boy."

I swallowed. and decided there was only room for a pure lie.

"I spoke to his secretary last week. He unexpectedly had to go abroad, and the agreement is that we will arrange a meeting ASAP, early next week. I'm on it, John, no worries."

"No, Harry, he's back…. I saw him yesterday at the golf court. "

I choked on my coffee.

"But I didn't want to speak to him before I knew for sure what the state of affairs was and when the appointment was…"

The coffee dripped slowly down the screen of my laptop.

"...Perhaps some heavy cats were being flogged here, and he had to return unexpectedly. So call again.."

Who is kidding here? I wondered as I dried my keyboard and screen with my handkerchief.

"Let me know something…. Please note that I will be in Paris on Monday and Tuesday; otherwise, I can make myself free. I'll talk to you."

I sat back in the leather armchair and sat staring into space for 5 minutes. I let a new Top 5 question bubble up to focus my thoughts on something positive. Ever since I read 'High Fidelity' by Nick Hornby a few years ago, compiling all kinds of Top 5s has been a favorite activity. Even when drawing up my professional alternatives list, I was inclined to limit myself to a Top 5. Until the moment of 'High Fidelity,' in my spare moments, or in the moments I created for that purpose... I had usually allowed myself to be seduced to searching eBay for all kinds of obscure albums, surfing the REM fansite, or playing 'cards' until the hearts and diamonds started to flutter before my eyes…

It's amazing how many different Top 5's one person can come up with. And at a certain point, you are even on the slopes of the Top 5 of the best Top 5s that you have made... There are also so many topics for which you can draw up a sensible Top 5. Of course, there are obvious topics such as music, film, or women/sex-related topics. And although these are the most obvious, those themes also remain inexhaustible.

The original top 5 of 'most beautiful women' had quickly evolved into sub-lists of the top 5 'Most beautiful secretaries', top 5 'Most beautiful female managers,' etc.

I had long thought that the market of women who would attract me was limited to the group of women with an upper age limit of 30 years or less. Even as a 16-year-old, I could have prancing fantasies about women who were a lot older. While I was furiously releasing the sticks on my drum set in 'The Future,' I dreamed away the thoughts of a pampering party with Hannah, the 25-year-old tap lady behind the counter. To my astonishment, however, I now had to conclude that I had apparently reached a point where I could also find women of 45 attractive. This was not only about the JLos or the Madonnas of this world but also about the female colleagues who looked good and had reached 40. I quickly managed to turn this observation into a positive interpretation by realizing that the market was actually getting bigger and bigger: the lower limit remained for approximately 18 years (... no, the physical beauty and attractiveness of our 17-year-old babysitter Virginie would not tempt me to adjust the lower limit... and besides, she would soon be 18.) while the upper limit apparently evolved along with my frame of reference. I have been wondering lately whether a time would come when I would set that upper limit once and for all... Let's be honest. There are just as many reasons to set the lower limit at 18. No compromise, and the upper limit at... at... er... 45?!

How banal... I kept surprising myself. My current Top 5 exercises did not have much to do with age, but still... The Top 5 of 'beautiful fellow mothers with 2 children.' This was embarrassing. How on earth did I come up with that? I tried to refocus my thoughts.

But Julie still looked damn good. Maybe there have been some tensions lately, but objectively speaking, I had to admit that she still looked damn good for her age and being the mother of 2 children. With the third pregnancy fully developed, I thought they were even more beautiful. No, my Top 5 wasn't actually that embarrassing after all. On reflection, it was quite a worthy Top 5 that at least paid attention to a significant group that might otherwise no longer appear in any list.

Were secretaries also eligible? Lisa was irrevocably in the Top 5. Maybe not number one, but still.

The list was written down on paper for me in no time. Ann, Lisa (so second.), Monique, Murielle, and Karen. How many mothers of 2, or at least I knew of, were in our agency? I would like to know that because now I was in danger of being subjective and might have excluded a number of them. I picked up the phone to dial the number of our HR representative, but then I realized that this question would inevitably raise too many questions... I hesitated.

"Hey, Harry...how was your weekend?"

I looked disturbed at Tom's weathered face. Tom...., what do you think about Tom? Tom, our marketing man, is the husband of fidgeting Jeannette, who maintains relations with the press and is responsible for large (local) marketing campaigns. But above all, he is an annoying guy who always comes up with the same jokes and then fills about 10 minutes of your time completely pointlessly. Now, I have nothing against weak talk, but it is always forced with Tom, and I wait impatiently for the moment he takes off. He is also the man who, on the one hand, provides the most crazy stories in the corridors and is a mood-maker. At the same time, the person who also knows the real news for the first time, such as Will and Diana... That struck me again when I saw his gaze on the A4 sheet... 'Top 5 mothers' was written above the names... I had put it in brackets (2 children). All that was missing was a hand-drawn ruler line underneath and a colon behind it. I scanned my desk with my eyes for a brochure or writing pad that I could place casually over the paper since removing the sheet and putting it in the Throwing the trash in the trash didn't seem like an option to me.

"I have an interesting article for you... from HRM.on-line. Maybe we should think about getting an interview with you in the next issue." Did everyone just act normal to me again? Will told me I should be ashamed and gave the impression that I had become personae non grata within Value Creators.

The article ended up at the top of my Top 5. Did it just seem that way, or had he placed that copy very emphatically in my Top 5? Tom winked and turned as a "Let me know" sounded.

The asshole. At least he had spared me some of his lame jokes. I quickly put my Top 5 in the inside pocket of my jacket and glanced at the HR article.

Seriously, I just couldn't manage to even read the introduction.

1. Tom, the marketing manager
2. Rob, the Director of the insurance division
3. Alex, the senior manager of the public sector division
4. Edgar, the senior manager of the insurance division
5. John, our own John...

Before I knew it, the names were scribbled on a tiny Post-it. I had learned my lesson! Ok, maybe Tom's number one position was a bit colored at the moment, but he would certainly fall into the Top 5 'most annoying male colleagues.' And the insurance division certainly had, in addition to the largest number of beautiful women, also by far the largest number of irritating men, without a doubt. Rob was absolutely the biggest asshole I knew. He was very full of himself and convinced of his charms with women. He also had an indefinable goatee and a sharply shaved mini mustache... You know how it is, a talking cunt. I somehow regarded Ed as an absolute outsider that could not be included in any list. He was the biggest bastard within Value Creators, and if there were ever a list of the 'number of victims behind the name,' he would be the winner with two fingers up his nose.

"Harry... eeh, Harry."

Melanie was standing at my desk.

"Am I interrupting? We had an appointment, right?"

Melanie, objectively the best Director, specialized in the implementation of HR processes. Melanie and I had been working together for about 5 years, perhaps also because no one else except Alex and me could put up with her. The question was how long that would take because I was convinced that she would also deal with me if it suited her. Yet, something in her made me respect her despite the harsh way she operated. She was a solid, dynamic woman with a good vision and a lot of autonomy, and she was not unsightly. Also, a woman who dared to argue with me when she thought I was wrong... Although I was doing well, I quickly knew that Melanie's star, just like Ed's, would rise faster than mine. When she started with us about

2 years ago, she was assigned to me for her first project. It was clear that she was hyper-ambitious but also really good. I was impressed and felt no threat from her, which may be my weakness for women, and in a way, we liked each other. Melanie was recently divorced. Melanie had one son... If Melanie had had 2 children, she would probably have made it into the top 5 'mothers of 2 children'. I tried to remember if Melanie had already been in a Top 5, and if so, which one... Now that I took in her, in her tight black trousers and leather vest, I was certainly there that she would be in the Top 5 of 'most beautiful divorcees' (even with and without a child...).

Until recently, Melanie was one of the few with whom I had had some kind of professional relationship of trust, and I think she also considered me a bit of a mentor. But that was all before the barbecue... You would think that some things had changed in our working relationship. Her opening sentence made me suspect that she needed an open conversation between two mature people who respect each other regardless of any unpleasant situations that may have arisen.

"No, you never interrupt, you know that..." (Hear yourself talking, I thought, while I couldn't remember anything about an appointment. This was about it).

Given my current 'etat d'esprit,' I was in favor of some off-the-record chatter.

I called Inge and had 2 coffees delivered.

"How was your weekend?" was the starting signal for me to elaborate on Barcelona in all its scents and colors.

I talked about my friendship with Fred and my visits to Barcelona; I talked about the Rambla and the nightclubs and almost sank into the low armchairs of La Vie en Rose.

Melanie faded in front of me as I dived back into the Spanish nightlife.

"Look, this is the conclusion I have come to." I saw my hand emphatically sticking the Post-it on the desk in front of Melanie. Apparently, I had switched, if not gone too far, from my Barca adventure to my Top 5 obsession without any embarrassment.

"I know it is a very subjective experience... what is the subject of the Top 5, how do you define that subject, and so on? But somewhere, I think there are shared opinions about certain Top 5's. You know me well enough. I think I know you a little, and we've been with the company long enough to be able to judge who is objectively the most annoying man at Value Creators Inc. are... Now, I think 'irritating' might not fully describe it. For me, it's actually also about the ugliest men, if I have to be honest. But now I am very curious about what nuances you would add to this Top 5?"

I sank back into my chair and looked at Melanie curiously, waiting for validation of my Top 5. This is a constructive attempt to repair any friction caused by my misconduct with Will. Starting with a clean slate.

In front of me sat a woman, transfixed... her eyes were bulging, and her mouth hung open. A look from a woman who had just returned home unexpectedly and caught her husband in bed, not with her best friend, but with her mother and brother, greedily enjoying this 'menage à trois'... A look from a woman who stood naked in front of the mirror in the morning and perceived a huge black male sex between her own legs... A look from a woman who had just been asked by the mouth of her crazy colleague about the top 5 'most annoying men within the company.'

It took me a while before I recognized Melanie in this woman. She collected herself and spoke to me:

"Haven't you really learned anything from the misery you caused at Will's party? What's wrong with you? Why all the frustration? I think you are mentally ill. It's only a matter of time before someone like you ends up in an asylum and even less time before Value Creators shows you the door. But I will wait quietly and do my duty because John called me this morning. We must prepare a final proposal for Spensers as soon as possible. John wants to force an appointment at the end of this week. He doesn't want to wait for your biweekly meetings with him anymore, and honestly, I understand why. So, from now on, we will work on it together in the meantime.

Now, it was my turn to come to grips.

AN EGG (IS NOT AN EGG)

Luckily we were able to arrange a single room. Julie didn't want to think about being in a room with others and being disturbed by the other patient's visitors. When I walked in, she was sleeping with a smile on her face and breathing calmly. I took Ben and Sam to my parents' house the night before.

"Why does mom have to go to the hospital?" Ben had asked. I decided not to go further than say, "Mommy has a lot of pain in the stomach, and the doctor needs to see if everything is okay." We had told them a few weeks earlier when the danger zone had formally passed, that Ben and Sam would have another brother or a sister. Ben was very excited, dragged all his toys out of the cupboard, and announced that he would show them all to his brother. We tried to correct him a few times, pointing out that the baby would be either a brother or a sister. Ben just wouldn't have accepted that.

"No, it's a little brother," he had shouted in a raised voice and had continued to repeat it, with the intensity and volume of the statement constantly increasing. The moment he had withdrawn into a corner crying, and we were convinced that he was trying to process his grief because he had understood that a sister might emerge, we were taken by surprise.

"If it's a sister, I'll make it a brother."

I decided that my further intervention would be misplaced and left the floor to the child psychiatrist on duty. Instead of elaborating on the possible gender of the new Jones, Julie began a lengthy yet clear and graphic explanation of the seed and the egg, ending with the apparently convincing statement that nature decides what the baby looks like. And whether it is a boy or a girl. Since then, the catchphrase of Ben and Sam, who until then did not seem to realize what the phenomenon of 'baby in the belly' meant, was 'it is nature that decides.' With that, the domestic peace in the family expansion was once again marked. Although the degree of my own maturity could be debated, and Julie could certainly make sharp analyses about it, I was convinced that as a future father, I currently understood and 'managed' it all much better than when we were happily expecting Ben. Actually, that was perhaps the most important difference: the feeling 'we are pregnant' was now very clear, while at the time of the embryo growing in Ben's abdomen, in my emotional world, there was no shared feeling of joy at all. I emotionally stood on the sidelines while Julie became happier every day of the pregnancy and had reactions and feelings that I could not identify, in many cases even found exaggerated or misplaced. I then also understood that 'nature had decided' that my ejaculated sperm could not swim around with impunity among all those eggs, there is no such thing as a free ride, and except for a concerned 'Shiiiiiiiiiiiit' when hearing about it, happy news, I didn't feel anything special. Yes, of course, Ben was the product of a well-considered choice, or at least that's what I kept telling myself because Julie could always convey that so convincingly, and we had had sex with each other with love, but the expected overwhelming feeling did not materialize. No fields or roads to be seen. Afterward, I caught myself with a slightly euphoric, proud male feeling, 'Look how fertile I am,' which I shared with my comrade by stroking his head. But that's where it all ended. If you were to ask Julie, in all honesty, what benefit she had from me during that period, she would rightly say that 'nothing' is the only answer.

In the first months after birth, the feeling of being 'excluded' only became worse. The whining 51-centimeter human being, who had initially presented himself in person through terrible contractions on a Tuesday morning, July 14, at 3.55 AM, and had seen the light through a cesarean section, received Julie's full attention. She was busy with him day and night. Breastfeed every 3 hours for 20 minutes. In my experience, they were 3-hour sucking sessions with 20-minute intervals. Changing diapers (boys, such a little one can shit), singing lullabies until the little one finally fell asleep only to be woken up by mom's finger in the mouth to see if the little one was still alive... Singing lullabies again.

I had no breasts on offer with which I could feed and seduce the little Jones. The problem was that Julie no longer paid attention to me, and I wasn't really allowed to interact much with little Ben. I was double offside. Whenever I was tempted to take the little owner in my arms and walk around the room with him or rock him to sleep, Julie immediately barked at me because he was in danger of getting a concussion. So, my strident sense of fatherhood was certainly not encouraged. I didn't really know what to do with the situation. Suddenly, I was not only living with a child psychiatrist but also with a primal mother and her own little wonder of the world. Sometimes, I almost literally pulled myself through the day.... Julie and I are becoming alienated from each other, and it is surprising how easy that is, even for a consultant with strong communication skills (that was the feedback I received from clients and evaluations) and a seasoned child psychiatrist. When I came home at night, as late as possible, I first hugged the bottle and then paid some attention to Julie and the little one. Every night, I went to bed with a light head, only to wake up in the morning with a heavy one, after which I got into my suit through a few shower jets and gave the mother of my child a kiss and the little one a pat on the head. And left. Since Julie lived in her own world, it took her a long time to realize what was going on. I was a stranger in my own home, within my own relationship, and cheated outside of it. Ultimately, masturbating as a couple is more fun as long as the tool is handled properly. It all started with the unexpectedly announced body painting session with Inge... After that, it was all over. But women are and remain women, mothers or not; sooner or later, you are screwed...

Around the sixth month, Julie returned to work after 4 months of maternity leave, which also confronted her with the world outside Ben; Julie started to bring me back. However, I did not really feel the need to give up the ground I had gained simply, so the many discussions we had and my regular argument, "You never pay attention to me.... You are only a mother... as a man, you have neglected me" was not sincere, out of a desire for rapprochement, but rather an excuse to secretly continue to mess around. Coming out of her stupor, Julie's intuitions were activated again, so it was only a matter of time before I had to admit to my sins. It was a lame but explicit text message from a certain Esther that the door had been closed. Julie had taken my cell phone when the message came in and read it. There wasn't too much fuss about it. That is, Julie waited and expected this to happen so that she would be proven right. Outside of a "See you bastard. I never want to see this again," no word was said at that moment. But the damage was done, therapy came into the picture, and trust was forever shattered. Forever.

After I sat at her bedside for 20 minutes, she woke up, turned her pale face toward me, and her smile gave way to tears.

"What did we do wrong, Harry?"

I don't deal well with questions of blame because they imply that you made mistakes in the process and that you could have controlled or manipulated the positive outcome. And automatically, the starting point was that we had been punished for a certain sin or stupidity that we had committed. I had committed countless sins, which had led to therapy because Julie wanted to give me a second chance, while she had indeed had every reason to punish me and throw me out. But here, in my opinion, we were dealing with a cruel example of 'nature deciding' over which we had no control whatsoever, and it would even be pretentious to think that it could have been otherwise. Seeing Julie lying there with the question of guilt written all over her face hurt me, and I deserved a heartfelt "God damn it."

I took her hand, which was connected to the IV.

"Julie, we did nothing wrong. We are just unlucky... The gynecologist has clearly indicated that we are not to blame."

If anyone had made a goddamn mistake, it was that bearded gnome.... I have now experienced several of those musselmen, and in my opinion, they are all strange birds, but what do you want when you see, feel, and smell plums all day? And I suspect they won't always be fresh.... In my opinion, you shouldn't romanticize that. From a professional perspective, it is almost inevitable that these guys always want to know what the woman in question 'carries' with her. Just as a consultant always wants to know how organizations and companies work in order to be able to make a diagnosis and make the right recommendations for improvements, and therefore cannot resist doing so in their private lives, I see such a cunt tinkerer always searching to the state of mind of the oysters present. Could such a guy in the female company also be able to smell whether menstruation is taking place or whether sex is taking place? I had wandered off a bit.

Not that I blamed our gynecologist for killing the embryo, but that he had firmly told us that everything was fine and it was 99.9% certain it was a girl. As a result, he had created a flesh-and-blood human being for us, which made the situation we were now confronted with unacceptable. Julie didn't notice my comment and fell back asleep sobbing. Her anesthesia had clearly not worn off yet, and if she woke up later, the situation would be even worse as, in addition to the physical pain, she would become even more aware of the life she had lost. It wasn't supposed to be. With this pregnancy, I had been there from the beginning, with all my consciousness and feelings. We were pregnant. What I had not felt with Ben, and as a result of our relationship almost ending, I had noticed more in myself when Sam was born. Sam was actually more of an accident than Ben in that we didn't talk about a second one, let alone think about plans. When Julie became pregnant with Ben, I felt taken by surprise because, despite the regular discussions Julie and I had about having children, or rather Julie's monologues and the announcement that she was stopping the pill, I realized the impact was clearly not. After about a month of being in therapy, our joint effort bore fruit as I apparently managed to channel my sexual urges back into my own relationship, resulting in a positive pregnancy test 7 months after Ben's birth.

The news was initially a huge shock. This announcement severely tested my wafer-thin belief that things would work out between Julie and me. I feared that after a love baby, which Ben clearly was, we would have created a relationship-saving baby that would signal the end of our marriage. How often do you hear couples with problems try to save what can be saved by having a child? The baby is a lifebuoy. With all due respect, that should actually be a punishable offense. Statistically speaking, I think this is the top category for divorced couples. After hearing the news, I was convinced that we had now reduced ourselves to a statistical number. Julie, who had a lot to do with statistics due to her study background and profession as a psychiatrist, saw this as the ultimate opportunity to join the exceptional cases within the graph of a Gaussian. So, working together, we struggled through the therapy and the pregnancy period with the common goal of making this a success. It did promote the process of my involvement in the pregnancy and the feeling of being a father. I also felt a change in Ben, who was no longer just a helpless creature but began to develop a will of his own, which could indeed be described as a father-son relationship. I actually felt pride and happiness in his development. Sam came into the world, and suddenly, the shitty diapers, bawling, you-must-be-quiet-because-he-sleeps-hours, sleepless nights, and supply of pacifiers doubled. In no time, we were revived, but miraculously, we managed to manage it all well as a tandem, and despite the enormous organization it entailed, there was hardly any stress. A beautiful period began during which we seemed to have found a balance, and we all found a place as husband and wife, father and mother, Ben and Sam. Then, not long after, my armpits started to leak uncontrollably out of a natural (or inspired by Catholic upbringing?) conviction that this was all too good to be true, that happiness could not last (2 years is already a very long time.) and life mainly meant misery. My current period at Value Creators was actually dramatic but not sad enough.

I was in a meeting with John to review the status of Spensers. Since Will set up these meetings, John and I met effectively every two weeks on Thursday afternoons. Progress with Spensers was fairly limited: Melanie, who had actually formally taken matters into her own hands, had actually managed to set up a new appointment with Eric Spensers and then another with his assistant Clara, whom I met during meetings with Eric. I had never seen her do anything other than frantically typing in the sentences dictated by her boss on her keyboard. I hadn't really insisted on coming along, so I left the sheep alone. Although I was confident that John would get the feedback sooner and first-hand, a crazy game was played where Melanie formally briefed me, and I then gave that feedback to John during the bi-weekly meeting. I had made it a hobby to make my feedback differ 180 degrees from Melanie's input. John didn't show anything. It was a farce that I managed to enjoy. Since I assumed that Melanie's account of the state of affairs was already far from reality, she had to assert herself a bit against that drunken, unhinged brat with his sweatshirts; I exaggerated everything even more. The potential deal had now been inflated to a 200 million Euro opportunity.

"We have to complete the business case by Friday and prepare a presentation for the next Board of Directors. I want to see that full phasing reflected in that."

I decided that making that presentation would be a job that Melanie could do.

"That's fine, John, it will be fine."

To my great surprise, I was asked to go to the meeting. And to my astonishment, that Friday afternoon at 4 PM, after Eric Spensers introduced us to the members of the Board of Directors and John, a limp Value Creators Inc. introduction story, left the floor to me to explain our proposal. Fuck, what was the point of this? Melanie sat stoically, staring into space with a grin. The sweat glands were reported immediately. "What is being waited for?" Eric shouted. John looked at me imperiously. This was a goddamn premeditated trap. It couldn't have been any other way, I suddenly realized. The two had deliberately played along to nail me to the cross here and in public, naive that I was

The customer would pass this on to the highest level, which meant that it would end up on Will's plate, who objectively held all the cards to throw me out without mercy. My possible means of blackmail did not really outweigh the trump card I had now played into their hands because, at this moment, 2 months after the funeral, who would attach any importance to a story about suicide that I had stirred up? Besides, Will may well have come clean to anyone who witnessed the barbecue and my sad exit there. As I realized with clarity what trap I had fallen into and with what consequences, a euphoric feeling replaced my original horror and discomfort. My armpits tightened again for an extra downpour, but this time from pure excitement. After all, the error of judgment that my friends at Value Creators had made was assuming that I was seriously concerned about my career at this fantastic consultancy company. And because of the process I had gone through, I had reached a point where I couldn't care less about any of it, absolutely nothing. Despite my appreciation of the earthly material things of life, which I could afford thanks to Value Creators, I was not afraid of alternatives. In fact, my future was undoubtedly far beyond Value Creators, and the only one who would be harmed was Value Creators itself, especially since Spensers had an important reputation in the market that would seriously damage our credibility based on this performance.

"Will we see any action? This is unworthy of Value Creators," Eric shouted. "I demand that a presentation be made now and your time be shortened to 20 minutes. The countdown has begun."

Now I'll play the game completely, I thought, got up and walked to the projector. At that moment, my cell phone started vibrating in my pants. I wriggled out the device to turn it off and saw Julie's number on the screen. Julie never called me during working hours, only if it was urgent. Given the situation and the irritated looks directed at me, it was not immediately convenient to answer the call, but what in God's name did I have to lose? It would only be a stay of execution... When I answered, Eric's "Enough is enough!" I was drowned out by my wife's flow of words and sobs.

"And... and... euuh... first it was a baby, then an egg, and now a problem. Harry... how is that possible?!"

From the sobbing, I concluded that it was not about the riddle of the day.

"He asked if I was sad but at the same time said that we should be happy that we already have two and that I should also understand that it is not easy for him either. He constantly has to deal with these kinds of cases, so very often, he is the bearer of bad news, but since he has been there from the beginning and he also considers them a bit like his children, it is also very difficult for him. A baby that is not a baby that no longer moves, whose heart is not beating, that is always very sad. Can you imagine experiencing that every day, while it is only once for me, because next time everything will go well, he said. And Harry, you know, intellectually, I understand that if there is a problem, there is, then there can be no baby and that that is better because nature usually does things as it should, and that interrupted pregnancies indicate a chromosome issue. And intellectually, I also know we learned that at university, it is probably an accident from conception. But I had also intellectually expected that such a chromosome problem would lead to some serious handicap, let's take Down Syndrome for convenience and that we would then receive bad news that would force us to make a difficult decision. What to do in such a case? Life with an abnormal child is not easy. I don't want to have any illusions about that, and it would be a very difficult decision, but Harry... there is no choice. The ultrasound showed nothing; we were fooled. No heart, no embryo, an egg dissolved in nothingness. And how do I explain that to Ben and Sam? They want a baby, not an egg. Ben wanted a brother; Sam didn't really know, but certainly not an empty egg. Harry, I don't know, that's going to be a trauma for the boys. Should I tell them that mommy is a magician who has a belly to perform disappearing acts... I will soon be going on tour with the big Winter Circus to play the magician in the arena night after night. And for you... you didn't want an egg either, did you?" Overwhelmed with tears, Julie suddenly fell silent for a moment.

My wife lost the pedals, I lost my job, and we lost our baby. That much was clear. It was not the time to say that everything was not too bad, but Julie regained her composure before I could say anything. In front of me, I saw Eric furiously gathering his things together. John apparently tried to calm things down a bit, but Melanie, who is a woman after all, seemed to be the only one who realized that something serious was going on. I pictured the scene like an audience member watching a silent movie.

"Until an hour ago, it was a baby, then an egg, and now nothing... But if it's nothing more, why do I have to go to the hospital? And what am I going to do between now and Monday, which is no less than 3 days? I never realized there are so many days between a Friday and a Monday... 3 Days. And if no baby or even an egg is left, what else is there to remove? Harry, Harry, are you still there? Why don't you say anything?"

Sobbing on the other end of the line. I had not had the impression that it would have been appropriate to give a verbal response. Now Julie seemed done with her part of the story, and it was my turn.

"Honey, I'm coming home… You're home, right? I'll be there in half an hour. Lie down quietly and try something."

I weighed my words with 'calm down' on the tip of my tongue. I knew there couldn't be a worse choice. John's heavy-handed grabbing and pulling on my tie broke the intimacy. The film suddenly had sound again.

"This will cost you dearly, friend."

"Julie, did you hear me? I'm coming now. I love you."

I hung up.

"Fuck, dude, do you really think I care."

My anger and tears were not played out, but I could not have chosen the drama in this setting better. Although sinking to my knees while crying might have made a little more impression, that would have been overacting.

"Friend, friend… What a ridiculous word; I hate it so much; what idiot came up with that, and what idiot uses it? Anyway, 'friend' would be completely misplaced in your case. I'm going home now; my wife had a miscarriage. Sorry to ruin your show, but I promise you, that was the last time."

"Harry, Harry, are you okay? Is everything okay with your wife and the child?" I heard Melanie shout as she ran after me through the hallway, where I quickly made my way to the exit.

If only I were deaf. My ability to control was put to the test again, with a negative result in advance.

The whole situation made it clear to me once again how big the fundamental difference between men and women actually is, and yes, I did indeed belong to the first category for the time being. Melanie, however, belongs to a special subcategory of woman, namely that of a retarded woman. All the respect I had ever felt for Melanie, I could hardly remember anything about it anyway, having been wiped out by her absurd comment just now. On the other hand, she was the only woman in the entire group, so her primal instincts kicked in when she realized something serious was going on. Something told her that she had to take care of me, that she had to care about this, despite the fact that she thought I was a terrible bastard, a pervert, who had descended to the lowest of the low... Since men and women fundamentally don't understand each other, why do you think relationships always take so damn much effort? However, she didn't feel like she should leave me alone. A difference of only about 14 centimeters, even in the raised position, designed in an appendage dangling between the legs, made a world of difference, and that would never be okay again.

"Miscarriage.... Baby.... Should I draw a picture of it?" I shouted. It was the first time in my life that I felt the urge to punch a woman. In high school, at the age of 16, in order to win the heart of a girl I was painfully in love with, I allowed myself to be seduced into a duel in the cafeteria. It had been a particularly pathetic display that left me with nothing except a torn wrist, broken jaw, and jeers. The lady in question had made it clear to me weeks before that there would be nothing between us, among other things, by making out in front of me at a school party with some jerk, who then proceeded to live up to his nickname as the Finger King. But I was convinced that my heroic act would turn the tide. Perhaps I would have been better off tackling the Finger King himself, to begin with, instead of the idiot from the class, and besides, my defeat also meant that I couldn't prove the validity of my belief anyway. In fact, here in front of Melanie, it was only the second time that I had the urge to use physical violence. So, I couldn't call myself a real guy. I managed to hold back, and my self-control was also helped a bit by the thought of Melanie's capabilities as a regional kickbox champion. Getting a huge beating from your female colleague must be the most humiliating thing a man can experience. Fortunately, the existence of fundamental differences between men and women means that in addition to feminine intuition, there is also such a thing as masculine logic. Right or wrong doesn't matter. My male logic made me decide not to respond anymore and to go to Julie as quickly as possible.

The weekend had been hell. Julie was badly affected and stayed in bed all weekend. That was good for her but extremely annoying for me. Suddenly, the full responsibility for the ins and outs of our offspring fell on my shoulders. I fully realized how much Julie did and could handle. Normally I don't wear anti-sweat shirts on the weekend, but I wear loose T-shirts. The same goes for today. At 10 AM, however, sweat poured all over my body, this time not because of a Value Creators event but because of the stress Ben and Sam generated. The men were awake at 7 AM. Julie had slept terribly and didn't wake up until around 5 PM. Moments before, she asked me, lying in my arms, my chest hairs wet from the many tears, if I would manage alone with the boys. I responded almost indignantly: "What do you mean? Can you make it… like 2 days? Is that hard?" To be honest, I feared the worst, and implicitly, by my reference to '2 days,' I had also admitted that it would take pain and effort to survive this. It wouldn't be anything more than survival. I dragged myself out of bed, cursing because I had downed a bottle of Gigondas the night before instead of the intended two glasses, resulting in a huge hangover. How difficult can breakfast actually be?

Ben started with 'Choco Pops,' a kind of fiber puffed in chocolate, then ordered me the 'Honey Corns' and then ordered the 'Classic Cruesli.' Each of these healthy fiber meals was mixed with a different dairy product. The first is milk, the second is low-fat organic yogurt, and the granola is strawberry yogurt. None of the three were eaten. A piece of gingerbread was what he used to sit in front of the television. Sam just wanted hot cocoa. That was quite a stroke of luck. However, the microwave threw a spanner in the works. Three minutes on the 1000 setting, with the cap on the cup, cause real havoc. I once read an article about an idiotic animal abuser who had exploded his cat in the microwave and quietly watched the entire process through a film camera that recorded the agony. I had never really been able to imagine it, but now, while I was trying to loosen the jet-black cake, scorched in the plastic with a chisel and sandpaper, I suddenly had a sickeningly clear idea of it. The chisel and sandpaper were not exactly the best tools for this job; I realized afterward when it turned out that there was visible permanent damage to the device. For some reason, the machine also stopped working on my second attempt to heat up a bottle of Nesquick. Sam enthusiastically encouraged him, who reinforced his support by accompanying every louder 'COCOA' cry for help with a thump from his plastic plate on the kitchen table. To save time, I filled the kettle with milk and cocoa, which would be much faster than simply boiling water in a pan on the gas stove. A minute later, I noted with some pride that my ingenious idea had worked. I proudly gave Sam the bottle that he greedily put to his throat. What do you do with all that cruesli, muesli and other supposedly healthy fiber junk mixed with milk and yogurt? All those lumps in a light brown or light pink substance looked disgusting. To me, the meat was still fish: it was not a purely liquid solution that you could simply pour down the gutter because that would cause blockages, and I wanted to avoid the consequences of that at all costs. It was also not a solid matter that you could just throw into the trash can, so what to do…? The only solution I saw was to use the toilet. Ultimately, the toilet was the right processing place when it came to meat and fish. Solid, rock-hard substance, released through a painful process, or rusty-brown gravy pushed forward. It all went through the same hole. I threw the various breakfast leftovers into the toilet and flushed. An exercise that was only moderately successful: several fiber remnants remained stubbornly attached to the edge of the pot, even after some brushing. Later that day, I tried to urinate a few things with a focused jet, but that was also to no avail.

After breakfast, I decided to drive to the woods to relieve Julie and please myself and the boys. On the way, we roared with Shakira, the only woman accompanying the 3 men. I was proud of my talents because they recognized the South American singer and, although using homemade word constructions, were able to sing along to the melody. In addition to Shakira, Madonna and Kylie were highly ranked. I was proud of my husband's preference for beautiful women; they did not make a big deal about age. In fact, they thought a bit about it along with their dad.

"Are we going to see deer?" Ben asked enthusiastically.

"I think that will be difficult because it is already late for the Bambis… they got up early when the sun rose to eat fresh, fresh, tender grass. Back then, you were still goofing off."

"No, not me," Sam reported, "I was awake and waiting for you. Because the bambis were waiting for us, now they are sad…."

I had had and lost enough arguments with Sam to recognize this situation. Sam was extremely passionate about creating his own reality and thus controlling every conversation. He usually succeeded, and if you as a parent were alert and creative enough to allow adult logic to prevail, you were repaid in full by a hysterical attack of screaming, crying, stomping, and pounding fists. One of the first times when that happened, I thought, 'That's why I married a child psychiatrist.' Julie decided to ostentatiously keep aloof after I told her so in so many words, leaving me with little more than to give in to Sam's version of reality finally.

"That's the stupidest thing you can do," said the child psychiatrist who had just informed me that she had the impression that she was married to one of her patients. "You have to give that boy a framework and make it clear that he cannot always manipulate every situation or conversation. He most likely does this because he has fears, and by controlling the content of discussions and the course of events, he tries to control that fear and eliminate any uncertainties."

"And where would that shortness of breath come from?" I asked with genuine interest.

"Ooh, that's definitely because of one of the parents. They may have suffered trauma during their youth, or perhaps have to deal with certain tensions within their relationship that they radiate to Sam."

"And so it's just one of us?" Why did I defensively ask that question rhetorically?

"Of course, you know that many psychologists and psychiatrists are known to be completely insane themselves," Julie replied, grinning. That's why I loved her.

"So it's your fault if the bambis are angry and don't come to see you," Sam continued.

"Yes, buddy, daddy overslept. If we do see a deer today or next time, I will say I'm sorry."

If Julie had been sitting next to me, she would have corrected me again, but I was on my own at this point and decided that I was doing a very good job, especially after Sam had kept quiet. Our eyes met in the rearview mirror, and I saw him implicitly admitting his defeat. Ben had fallen asleep, dreaming about meeting the Bambis. The piece of forest we drove to consisted of a hilly patchwork where areas of forest alternated with open, elongated meadows. I had been coming there with my father since I was young, from Sam's age now. Even though time passes so scandalously fast and the world is more fluid than ever, it's amazing how certain traditions and locations remain untouched as a kind of safe haven for souls in danger of being lost. Simple things such as the football world championships, the annual Christmas party, car washes, and this piece of nature- some elements of life always remain the same. The path I took, which we called the '3rd path' as it was preceded by two other forest paths from the road, from the direction we came, was still in the same condition as it was 30 years ago. As a little boy, I excitedly counted up to the 'third path,' after which the big adventure began. The same route again and again, and usually deer or roe deer in the same place, grazing in the grass, as if we had made tacit agreements before our meeting. But the familiar image had never gotten boring, and even now, I felt the tension with every new vista that emerged. Would there be? How many? Would they see us and run? The '3rd path' was equivalent to Long John Baldry's 'Morning Dew,' a world hit in my 9-year-old experience (and I was right!), which played softly on the radio on the way to the big adventure.

However, we were late today, so expectations were low, and I let the boys sleep until I parked the car. Luckily, I had put boots on them so they could fully enjoy themselves.

In no time, they were high in a pine tree where an abandoned blackbird nest, with two broken blue eggs left behind, was discovered.

"Where did mommy go?" Sam asked.

"I think a cat or magpie chased away the mother," I said.

"Where have the little birds gone?" Ben looked at me questioningly.

"Maybe one or two have fledged, but there were no babies in these two eggs," I said after I saw the gunk in the eggs. The experience of a peaceful and pure moment between father and sons was short-lived because Daddy turned out not to have brought any food, drinks, or toilet paper. These are standard parts of the survival kit that Mom apparently always carried with her.

"Dad, I'm thirsty," "Dad, I want gravy," "Hungry," "HUNGER!" "I want a waffle," "I need kaka!" the whole arsenal was discussed, and every time, I was left empty-handed, which stirred up the whining and whining. The primal needs of eating, drinking, and defecating swept away interest in any game. Despite the clamor for food and drink, I blamed myself most for the lack of toilet paper because I wasn't really eager to lead the 'dirty hands operation.' I tried to limit the damage with the necessary grass, but that only resulted in a mess with a number of stray green blades.

More than ever, I realized Julie's indispensability. We returned home exhausted, with smelly hands and starving, whining boys in the backseat. I was exhausted.

Towards the evening, I decided to use the rough tools to clean up our toilet. I wanted to avoid at all costs that Julie would have the opportunity to correct me, which would confirm to her that I couldn't handle it all on my own, so all possible traces had to be erased. At 8:30 PM, I put the boys to bed, read them a Winnie the Pooh story, and evaluated the past day with them. They had enjoyed it with Daddy, but they missed Mommy too. They had been washed, in their pajamas and in stocking feet, and they had crept into our bedroom to give Mom, who seemed completely out of the world, a kiss. In their own bed, they listened attentively to my reading talents. I gave them a kiss and told them I loved them and that they should sleep well.

"Daddy…" Sam started, slightly whining. "Dad, you know what? If you die, we will be very sad and cry. Right, Ben?"

Ben confirmed hotly.

"That's good, but Daddy isn't going to die anytime soon, guys," I said soothingly.

"Nooooooooo," said Sam.

I crawled off the bed after going through his pacifier collection with Sam to make sure we had placed the right ones between his teeth. I had turned off the light and was already standing on the stairs when Sam whispered loudly enough, "Daddy, but if Mommy dies…. Then we cry even harder." I decided it was worth following Sam's reasoning a little longer. I walked back to their room.

"Oooh, Sam, why are you crying so much louder?"

"Because mom knows everything and can do everything."

So, after a day of effort during which I had spared no expense, prevented disasters, and been the ideal father, it was a bit of a pill to swallow. My position within the Jones household was clear. And they were right... I had failed, putting Julie's indispensability on full display. Sam lay on his side, closed his eyes, and fell asleep contentedly to join his brother in dreamland.

I went downstairs to our utility room to gather some cleaning supplies. I wanted to make something right and really surprise Julie. While Emmylou Harris stimulated me with her Daniel Lanois-produced 'Wrecking Ball', I scrubbed the entire living room and kitchen, cleaned the sink, and ventured to the toilet. I took a new bucket from the pantry cupboard as the other one was now filled with muddy water. At the bottom of the green bucket, I saw the remains of a white emulsion. When I poured the all-purpose cleaner into the bucket, the white stuff bubbled a bit and then turned blue. I decided to stick my nose deep into the bucket in a reflex that a chemist, or any other normal thinking person, would not have or at least suppress.

The next moment, I fell forward against the floor, gasping for breath as blood poured from my nose and hammered my head. Breathe, I had to keep breathing. 'Gasp for breath,' I suddenly knew exactly what it meant. Imagine that, as a woman, you have to explain that you have lost both your unborn child and your husband in 24 hours. The cause of your baby's death is slightly confusing but plausible, and you end up hearing it so often. But the cause of your husband's death died while removing cruesli remains in the toilet. That would be a little more difficult. I dragged myself through the hallway. There was no shouting as I had to try to get air. Violently moving purple spots danced before my eyes, causing me to misjudge the position of the passage to the living room and hit my head head-on on the door frame. The purple spots became black spots and yellow stars. I felt my way further through the living room to the kitchen. Water… I wanted water on my face and also to drink as if I could swallow the shortness of breath. With all my strength, I pulled myself up from the counter. I thought there was no point in calling a doctor because I couldn't talk. That would take too much energy and could mean my death. For the next few minutes, which felt like hours, I let water from the tap flow through my hair and down my face. The stream of blood from my nose mixed in a whirlpool with the water around the drain. I couldn't imagine Julie catching me now. In her state, finding me in this situation wouldn't do. And there was no way I could explain it. A chemical reaction had occurred in a green plastic bucket, and the poison raced through my body to fatally affect my system. The sense of time disappeared; there was only now, now, now, now… I wondered if I had ever known another moment. Presumably, you only reach the highest state of present experience when you feel the hot breath of death on your neck. I know plenty of people who believe that the Carpe Diem philosophy of life is a good approach, but here and now, in this death throes, I knew that it was an unrealistic and pretentious pursuit. My heart was beating like crazy, which was accompanied by enormous pain. The search for alternatives for my career will come to an abrupt end here, I feared. A mirror hangs above the sink. I saw a man with panic and fear in his eyes. He was completely unprepared for what had happened, what was to come, and why he should.

Never symptoms of old age, no organized trips, no scary cancers that would exhaust the body and make it waste away, no incontinence diapers, no dementia, no nurses who had to come and wash the powerless, tired body, no bedsore symptoms, no further questions, no more guilt complexes.

And yet, there was no sense of my life passing before me in a flash that told me that it wasn't over yet, that I was really in a battle with death and had not yet finally lost.

Poison, poison… I remembered from my mother, one of her many wisdoms, that drinking milk could cause such a reaction in the stomach that all misery would be released. And since I had nothing left to lose, I put my money where my mouth was. Spluttering, gasping for oxygen between gulps, I drank the milk in large gulps. Somehow, I was convinced that less than 1 liter wouldn't be enough, so I drank the whole carton. It didn't take long before I started feeling even worse, which gave me hope. The way to the toilet turned out to be too long because when I opened the door to the hallway, the first eruption found a way out.

A form of liquid white grit that never ended. I was turned inside out to expel the end from my body. The misery continued to come in waves. Death slowly dripped from the door, leaving white specks on the dark oak. My head rested against the wall. I felt like everything in my body was slowly but surely starting to fall back into place. In my experience, I stood there for hours waiting for the sign that everything was over. The moment Julie appeared in my mind made me realize it was over. The clock on the dresser showed 11:48 PM. For about 5 minutes, I sat with my head in my hands, staring into space and recovering from this intense experience. Despite the fact that I felt weak, but actually surprisingly good given the experience I had just had, I knew I had to take action. Just as the traces of impending death had been expelled from my body, the external remains had to be removed. I flushed the bucket of deadly poison down the toilet. I emptied the other bucket of dirty residual water in the kitchen, refilled it with hot water, and added standard dish soap. That had to be enough.

Exhausted, I collapsed on the couch. 00:23. The job was done. I thought about Julie, the boys, myself, us... Despite, or precisely because of, my soaked shirt, a grueling, almost fatal day for myself, during which I constantly cursed and ranted, internally or otherwise, I felt intensely happy while everyone was sleeping. Perhaps the cynical part was that I experienced that blissful feeling when I was alone with myself while they were all sleeping, and I had been continuously cursing my family situation and all its burdens during the day without managing the problem. At the same time, there was no way Julie was happy right now. She lay deathly ill because of the lost life on her bed, waiting for Monday, the day of redemption.

Richard Ashcroft sang in the background about 'I get my beat,' a beautiful song from his unsurpassed first solo CD 'Alone With Everybody' with a slightly melancholic hint that took me to a 'Top 5 Most Melancholic Songs'. It's not difficult, although I would prefer to put together a melancholic Top 30 that would make me less limited.

1. Hymns to the Silence, Van Morrisson
2. April 5th, Talk Talk
3. From the Morning, Nick Drake
4. Nightswimming, REM
5. Once, The Hunters

They were allowed to put it, burned on a CD, in my coffin so that I could completely immerse myself in it in moments of loneliness and sadness. A bit corny, perhaps, but 'Childhood Dreams' by Nelly Furtado can also be included if it is noted. Partly because of the dramatic bombastic organ work at the song's beginning. I associate organs with churches, and I associate churches with my parents and my youth. Associations can be that simple.

Julie was back on Sunday. We didn't really talk about what had happened to us. We both tried to give substance to the harmonious family by devoting all our attention and energy to Ben and Sam. Around 5:00 PM, I drove to my parents' house to drop off the boys for the night. "Maybe the baby in mommy's belly is sick, and then there will be no brother or sister," Ben remarked when we said goodbye. It is often astonishing how children fully understand the truth and can express it perfectly in a simple way, while we, as sensible adults, go out of our way to disguise or unnecessarily nuance the reality. I gave him a kiss, whispered that maybe he was right, hugged Sam, and left.

This morning, we drove to the hospital, where we had an appointment with the gnome. A friendly smile on his annoying face, but I had decided to hold back and not unnecessarily increase the stress for Julie.

"This phenomenon involves an empty egg, also called an 'oeuf blanc,' which amounts to an error in conception that means the fruit can never be viable. Fortunately, nature solves this itself."

My unprecedented control prevented me from asking the gynecologist questions about lime and Easter eggs. Julie's resistance was so low that a discussion about his error in judgment - he had said everything was fine! - it would be completely inappropriate at this point.

20 minutes later, I saw Julie in bed, accompanied by two nurses, driving away from me and down the hallway. Before she disappeared behind the wide doors, her right hand waved weakly in my direction.

I collapsed on the couch in the waiting room and resolved to quickly do something else with my life and to stay with Julie, the woman of my life, forever.

JOYCE

Okay, there are those moments when the flesh is weak, which any reasonable person would expect. Not because there is necessarily alcohol involved or a marital dispute, but simply because the woman is the woman, at least at that moment and at least for that one time. And it may not even be a matter of the flesh offering little resistance but rather a total 'click' or a fatal combination of the two. It can happen to anyone, at least if you're not a romantic lost soul who believes in the "one and only." I was once such an illusionist myself. Fortunately, it was a long time ago, but until I was 22 years old, that was the ultimate goal: to find the one and only and not make any compromises about it. There are few events or actions that I regret, including my misconduct, within Value Creators Inc. because that's how I like to classify it, but I do regret all those missed opportunities under the guise of pathetic moral chivalry. All those opportunities I missed led to nothing except pure frustration, for which I would pay the bill sooner or later. In retrospect, that moment must have happened around the age of 22, as I let Jane grab me mercilessly at a student party. A giant of a woman, where everything about her was several sizes too large, making it possible with a healthy dose of imagination to justify the act afterward due to the proportionally correct ratios. But she wasn't particularly attractive, to say the least; she was downright ugly, and she didn't have an appealing personality either. The only thing we had in common, besides an uncontrollable sexual urge that needed to be expressed, was a shared interest in The Hunters, to whose 'Easy Going' we were grinding against each other on the dance floor. It had been clear from the beginning, when Fred introduced me to her, that I would end up on top of her. Or she would be on top of me. Sometimes, I still wake up screaming at the moment when she plants herself with that enormous rear and overgrown reception area—bikini lines were unfortunately not yet common—on my face while I'm lying in the wet grass with my jeans around my knees, at the ready. It wasn't honey I tasted on my tongue. Thankfully, that nightmare doesn't happen very often, but it's a phenomenon that has occurred so frequently since being with Julie that she demanded an explanation. Haltingly, I explained my trauma about my 'Statistics' exams that I barely passed, but in my dreams, I failed again, meaning I had to retake the exam for the umpteenth time. The child psychiatrist found that to be a plausible explanation.

Although I could only handle the imposing chassis with my eyes closed, the act with Jane actually opened my eyes. All that bullshit about the one and only one that I had been clinging to was pointless, and it hadn't brought me any closer to the one that I had met at 18 during my last year of high school. Christine was beautiful, and I immediately put her on a pedestal. She's the only blonde woman I've fallen for, so that should have rang a bell; her appearance completely blinded me. I loved everything about her, including when she spoke, when she didn't speak, when she embarrassed me, when she flirted with others, and when she got hit on at parties. It didn't matter at all. She was meant for me; one day, she would be mine. In the meantime, I also gave others a break. I reached my own highlights with do-it-yourself practices and Christine in mind. Eventually, it got boring, and with Christine not an inch closer within reach and Jane's impressive body on offer, I went to my knees.

The period after this dramatic excess was one of nightmares in which Jane continued to harass me, combined with a search through the female carnal paradise for balance in my relationships with ladies. The real after-effects of my delayed puberty had arrived a few months after Julie's contractions had led to Ben's eventual cesarean section delivery. The enriching experience with the Agnesses and Munas of this world (and the therapy with a child psychiatrist and a relationship psychologist) has given me a few new insights:

One: sex with women is sex with women. Whether it is with a small, chubby brunette with an Italian accent, a dark blonde slender German, or a busty black gazelle from Zambia, whether it's soft sex with over-extended foreplay or really hard sex on a kitchen table strewn with fruit and vegetables, whether it's her faked orgasms or not (as long as there's screaming), sex is sex. Based on that philosophy, you might as well limit sex with a partner to your own relationship rather than continuing to freewheel without the risks of all kinds of scary, fatal, or otherwise diseases and unwanted pregnancies.

Secondly, sex never gets old. A not-insignificant killer. The basic principle here is that it concerns sex with yourself or sex with one or more women. Sex with men, except with myself, and that is honestly not quite the same, I suppose, has never spontaneously occurred to me and does not belong to the category 'what you should do at least once before you die.' Sex with other specimens is completely ignored.

But the catch is that sex with the same woman can get boring. Because even though sex is sex (a whistle is a whistle, a pussy is a pussy), a lack of imagination and variety can lead to a rut, and if you get sucked into it, you are more likely to question the validity of the first lesson ("Yes, but a Japanese tongue really licks differently than a French one") to put it to the test again. Julie understood that well, especially after we had been in therapy. And had she also concluded that sex with the same man could also become boring? That thought, especially since I was the man in question, took me by surprise. It's intriguing, but the men I know, including Harry Jones, tend to think that the enormous, widely described, and acknowledged differences between men and women mean that all experiences, beliefs, and perceptions that men have about relationships and sex are automatically different from the experiences of women. Wrong. Men think about sex more often; men are more physically oriented, and men cannot do several things at the same time. All correct, but (unfortunately) that does not mean that no aspects apply to both sexes. Where do I get the nerve and pretense to believe that Julie would never cheat? Why wouldn't Julie also experience that sex with men is sex with men? And if the answer to the questions is positive, the big scary difference may be precisely in the fact that different conclusions are drawn. Imagine that Julie draws the conclusion from the same lesson that she, therefore, has 'carte blanche' to cheat. And why not?

Although it was after a significant sample size (I know my statistics), I had eventually concluded that I would only 'indulge' my sexual urges (wild sex instead of foreplay) with Julie and would no longer be distracted by other female beauty. In the first few months after Ben's birth, Julie paid no attention to me at all, and I used that as an excuse for my escapades, but even when she started seeking me out again, and we were in therapy, she wasn't always in the mood for the act. Now, to be honest, I can imagine that your desire automatically fades when you know and feel that your husband is happily engaging in affairs while you're at home waiting for him. In any case, with Ben as a weak excuse, we had come to explicitly discuss our problem. And then, fortunately, Julie brought out all her creativity to keep our sex life varied and exciting, to avoid monotony. For my birthday, I received a hefty edition of the Kama Sutra, with beautiful photos of a couple in full glory demonstrating all the positions that the Indian sage Mallanaga Vatsyayana had devised. The

Kama Sutra, or Kama Shastra, was likely written around the 4th century AD and presents various erotic subjects in a didactic manner. Indeed, not all 35 chapters in 7 parts are about straightforward sex; some parts are devoted to love in general, courtship, and marriage, but my 10 favorite chapters are about 'sexual union,' providing a detailed description supplemented with delightful photos of various sexual techniques, from kissing through foreplay to orgasm, covering all kinds of positions and threesomes. I thought it was a nice gift and enjoyed leafing through it for inspiration while Julie did her prep work in the shower, which often involved turning the book into different positions to see the right complexity. However, the spouses had different ideas about the use of the book. A source of inspiration for me, a manual for Julie, except for the trios, as it turned out. And since Julie's will is law in the Jones house, I regularly found myself in awkward positions where I had to imagine turning the photo in different directions in order to understand how our bodies were intertwined and where to place my left foot or right hand.

A few times, I was struck by terrible cramps in the calves where Julie misinterpreted my screams as a new dimension to my experience of pleasure. Apparently, this led to ecstasy for Julie because the intensity of her sliding and the rubbing of our genitals intensified, which made my contraction even worse. Julie usually experienced an absolute climax (no, not 'faked') while the bed thundered. Another time, I was hanging between the bed and a chair, like some kind of walkway in the jungle, and all sorts of things were happening to my gender while, in my perception, Julie was sitting on the other side of the bed. My flexibility played tricks on me here, and the score was rudely interrupted by the chair falling back against the mirror wall under my leaning weight. But hey, one learns by doing, and it must be said that Vatsyayana's vision certainly brightened up our sex life.

Julie agreed that the blue turban looked a bit absurd and didn't always promote excitement, so we dropped it after a few tries. In addition to the Kama Sutra, Julie also purchased all kinds of lingerie and relaxation items, such as massage oil and special massage tools. Very simple remedies but effective.

In no time, Julie was pregnant with our second son, Sam.

Recently, after the miscarriage of what would have been our third, we went through a new sexual crisis, namely that of teetotalism, because Julie was currently living mainly in her own world in which things had to be put in order, and there was no room for sexual relations.

Lesson 3, and the most painful: once your wife suspects marital irregularities (and the female intuition tells you she is right even though you try to deny it to yourself), there is a dent in trust. that will never be fully restored. A certain form of distrust is viable; partners can even regard it as an accepted weakness within the relationship. However, it is not a fixed amount of suspicion that you can place in a small box as a decoration object for your wedding. It lives like a piece of wood, shrinking or expanding depending on the season. If it expands too much and breaks out of the joints, you will have to do serious renovation work or complete replacement work. At times that were unexpected for me, Julie's suspicion was so great that it paralyzed our relationship, and I felt forced to tell half-truths, withhold facts, or simply lie about the smallest details that had nothing to do with excesses outside the home. But suddenly, everything was suspicious, every phone call, every text message, every late return home. Account statements were scrutinized, comments about colleagues were investigated to see if any female silhouette was visible, and I had completely paranoid tendencies for which I was to blame. Distrust is the latent rot within a relationship. So I made up male team members and customers, stored male names in my phone directory and had mock conversations with Jim, Jeff, and Paul. Working for a female client raised all alarm bells; working with a team of female colleagues was limited to solo work or a purely male affair. But a team 'dinner' was then viewed with suspicion because the men might then go hunting or be tempted into placing €50 notes with their teeth between their breasts in a pole dancing tent. I ordered a bouquet of flowers for a sick customer, an HR director who was out of action for 2 months due to the removal of her uterus, so I thought it was only professional to wish her a recovery sincerely. But since it involved the combination of 'female customer' with a 'bouquet of flowers,' I could never have that explained credibly. I decided to keep quiet about the whole event, which was beyond Julie's detective instincts. One evening, the account statement with the debit in question was on my pillow. "And what is that?" she asked. That sentence said it all. It assumed that her husband's secret life was behind closed doors between open legs and that it did not belong to Julie. And in that sense, there was also the assumption that it would only be a matter of time before she caught me. Because she was going to find the proof, that piece of evidence was now before me. I felt powerless, and my response was silence. What else could I say now? Telling the truth would seem unbelievable because why had I not told it before, and if there was nothing wrong, why did I have to keep it hidden? A vicious circle that I had started to draw myself: no herb against crops. I knew I had to live with it within the relationship and try to manage Julie's volatility in the hope that it would never reach such proportions that she would send me out or close the door behind her.

And yet, there are times when the flesh is weak, when a reasonable person cannot expect otherwise despite lessons learned. It happened to me.

I had been driving around in my cocoon for days, or was it weeks, listening to music, standing leisurely in traffic jams, and watching drivers get excited to no end, blowing their horns and swearing at each other. All very entertaining. I witnessed the worst examples of road rage. It turned out that it was not just aggressiveness that provoked violence. One day, I was quietly standing in a traffic jam, enjoying the sounds of Peter Gabriel's 'Love to be Loved.' I was completely absorbed in the song that I had essentially rediscovered as one of the best but least-known songs from 'Us.' The cool rhythm generated by subtle percussion supplemented with Gabriel's voice sounded phenomenal through my 12 speakers... The climax of the song starts at 3 minutes 33 and still gives me goosebumps.

"And I let go,

And I let go,

I couldn't let go of it.

Though it takes all the strengths in me,

And all the world can see,

I am losing such an essential part of me.

I can't let go of it,

You know, I mean it;

You know, I mean it.

I recognize how much I have lost,

but I cannot face the cost.

Cause I love to be loved,

Yes, I love to be loved;

I love to be loved,

Yes, I love to be loved,

I love to be loved,

Yes, I love to be loved…"

While I was sitting there enjoying life in my cocoon, safely shielded from the real world, I saw the man in the car to the right of me get out of his car and head towards me. He was bald and short; I think he was about six feet tall and had a round redhead with an out-of-proportionate nose. His pants were short, making him look even smaller; he wore a blue oversized shirt with a bright red tie and had a heavy gold link bracelet on the right wrist. The eyes looking at me through the window were watery blue. The nose pressed against the glass looked unappetizing. The tapping of his bracelet against the window interrupted my blissful moment.

I tried to ignore him, but that was out of the question. He now also tapped the windshield with his left hand. Now, get something, I thought. With the music at the same loud volume, I lowered my window a bit. I put my hand behind the shell of my ear to hear what the good man had to say. I gestured that I couldn't understand. Based on the flaring and expanding of his enormous nostrils and foaming at the mouth, from which I concluded that he was reaching a boiling point that was inexplicable to me while snorting, I decided to put my stereo on 'pause.' The fact that the guy now started pulling on my window with both hands also played a role. The sudden silence took him by surprise, and he immediately let go.

"What's gotten into you?" I asked calmly.

"You're sitting here so calmly in your car, smiling into the distance. Is this fucking fun. Every morning I get stuck in that endless fucking traffic jam, and the gentleman just sits quietly in his car, whistling. Unemployed or something? I work my ass off, which is no laughing matter anyway, then I'm stuck in a traffic jam, and there's this grinning idiot next to me." I understood that I was the direct object of that sentence.

Well, I honestly didn't know how to respond. Apparently, my choice was not the right one.

"Eeeuh, I can advise you to listen to Peter Gabriel, for example." I showed him the CD cover of 'US.' "Of course, I don't know what kind of installation you have in your car, but in general, it is relaxing music."

With one elbow bump, my left side window flew in and landed on my lap. Apparently, that was enough relief because he turned around resolutely and walked back to his car.

The frustration expressed completely escaped me.

Besides my physical absence, I tried to avoid any other form of contact with Value Creators, which I usually succeeded in because there was not much communication with me after the Spensers affair.

The week after the disastrous steering group and Julie's miscarriage, I was summoned to Will's office. "Jones, upstairs in 5 minutes," the horn blared. I had not seen or felt Will since the conscious punch. I was prepared for anything and had resolved to repay physical assault in the same coin. To reinforce that intention, I had a brass knuckle in my right trouser pocket. Not a real one, but a plastic one that Ben had received in some 'gangster' gift set for his birthday. I briefly considered taking the handcuffs and the gun, but that seemed a bit excessive. The brass knuckles looked very real, and if there was a scuffle, I could threaten it or use it effectively. Getting a strip of sharp plastic on your face had to cause quite a bit of misery.

With his feet on the desk, Will sat back in his black leather chair.

"Sit down, Harry. How is it going?"

Although I was asked the question and wanted to answer, I felt it was better not to give a verbal response.

"Listen, Harry, we spoke a while ago with clear agreements regarding Spensers and reporting to John. The feedback I received via the customer." When he said the last words, he pulled his legs off the table, returned to a sitting position, and now pointed in my direction. "…That things don't look so rosy. And now I express myself euphemistically." The volume of his voice increased as the veins in his neck began to swell. I dug around in my pocket, looking for the brass knuckles.

"According to John and Melanie's estimate, the chance of winning is less than 10%, and the value is less than €2 million instead of €200. And they certainly don't know when that godforsaken shitty contract will even come into being." Meanwhile, Will was pacing around his office, sometimes standing still at the window and talking, looking into infinity. The spots on the back of his neck crept up from under his shirt collar, which was so tight around the neck that you wondered if there was any space between them to slip under.

"Don't look at me like that. You dug your own grave. You have to get out. There's nothing more that can be done. We will respect your notice period so that you can look for alternatives."

Will stared at me silently, indicating that he now expected my response. I continued to look at him calmly without opening my mouth.

"Have you lost your tongue, Jones? That's something new!!"

"I just lost my job. That's not a complete surprise to me, so what else should I answer?"

I stood up quietly, slid my chair under the desk, and turned to the door to leave the office.

"Hey, hey… you can't just walk away. I called you here for a meeting."

"I don't really like the dialogue, Will; you let me come here because you have found a way to banish me permanently, and you have already forgotten about your wife's suicide, remember? Because that was a few months ago. The possible revelation of reality, which could lead to a scandal around your own person, no longer inspires you with fear, at least not when it comes to the damage it could cause you professionally to the outside world. I cannot imagine that a flesh and blood person, no matter how dull, does not have a little voice somewhere in the back of his head that whispers to him, 'guilty, guilty, guilty.' Softly, buzzing, like a bothersome mosquito that just keeps coming back."

Beng!

Goddammit, he did it again.

I lay on the floor, feeling my jaw as Will stood over me.

"You may continue to use our facilities, but I warn you, if you make a fuss in any way, I will have you thrown out. We have enough resources and good lawyers to get our justice in the event of a lawsuit, so don't have too many illusions."

I haven't had any illusions for a long time now. It was self-evident that I had to look for something else; I had already come to that realization myself, and the process was now just accelerated.

I scrambled to my feet. I decided to leave the brass knuckles untouched.

"Will, I think it's all fine this way." I turned and left his office.

And so the phone call had taken me by surprise.

"Is that Harry?" a friendly, pleasant English female voice as I guided my Bertone along narrow roads through the hinterland.

"Hi, I'm Joyce from the London agency. I came to you through... I am currently working on a huge outsourcing deal at UK Telecom and am looking for best practices in terms of possible scenarios and also a sounding board. Someone who can help me with the business case. I will be at your office the day after tomorrow for other reasons and was wondering if we could meet."

I wanted to talk about leaky armpits, barbecues, suicide, punches... but decided: "That seems fine to me. What time are you available?"

"I'll be arriving at the airport at 10 AM, so we'll either meet for lunch or afterward."

"You know what, I'll pick you up from the airport after I take the kids to their school. How do I recognize you?"

"Ooh, that's very kind. You recognize me by a large blue Value Creators travel bag."

"Perfect Joyce, see you then."

No reason to be in a dark mood.

Estimating my current score on the trust meter, I decided to tell Julie about what might be my last professional act for Value Creators. Julie responded moderately, "Why do you have to get it from the airport if necessary? She can take a taxi, right?"

I left out the 'saving time' argument.

A fresh open look, large brown almond-shaped eyes, loose short straw blond hair above the shoulders. A white blouse, under a red leather jacket, tucked into high black smooth leather boots with high heels above tight black pants. A Value Creators travel bag. That was Joyce. She was small, about 5'5 feet tall, I guessed, and about my age. A firm handshake. And from then on, I knew. My heart was in overdrive, beating at a rhythm I had never felt on my exercise bike, even on the steepest climb. I had brought the Bertone out of the stable for the occasion, which made an impression. From the moment we joined hands as an introductory greeting, I approached Joyce as if I had to woo her as if I had secured a date, but the woman in question still had to be conquered, knowing full well that she was open to it, that that was the expectation. I wanted to drive away with her to the horizon, away from everything and everyone, here and now.

"What a beautiful car… With this, your children will be proud when you deliver them to school."

She remembered that I had children, or was it a smart move because she saw the two high chairs in the back?

"Is their school far from the airport? How old are they? A boy and a girl?"

I answered all her questions. Her legs were crossed, the leather jacket lay on Sam's high chair, and her white shirt had two buttons open, showing a beautiful cleavage and beautiful neck around which hung a subtly exotic matte silver necklace. I had put on a Mosquito Bar lounge playlist.

It was time for my question period. Joyce originally came from Ireland, moved to London when she was three, where she has lived ever since, 35 years ago. My age! Two children, Liam, a boy of 8 and a girl, Deirdre, 4 years old. My eyes slid over her slender hands with long fingers and beautifully manicured dark red nails. Lots of rings, but no wedding ring, I thought. My analysis was confirmed without being asked.

"My husband Kevin, an Irishman, wasn't really interested in having children… He left me alone one evening after Deirdre, which was actually an accident. "I'm leaving," he said, taking his bags and leaving. Never seen or heard from again. Do you understand that… I sometimes wonder what goes on in a man's psyche."

"I wonder that all the time," I replied. A disarming smile. "You're funny."

That was correct, although I haven't consciously drawn that card yet.

"Are you married?" the question cut through me like a knife. And why wouldn't she ask?

"Yes... yes, I am married to Julie...For years now." It sounded idiotic to me 'for years'... what was that supposed to imply? Joyce asked no further questions and started talking about the real reason for her visit and our appointment. She briefed me on the situation of UK Telecom, her assessment of the deal opportunities, the relationships she had built with the customer, and the successful visit she had also made to our center in Budapest. If she were to succeed in selling this deal, she would be promoted to Director. She beamed at the thought of that well-deserved next step. Like me, she was a product of Value Creators Inc. We knew nothing other than the narrow world of our own company and, as such, had no other reference. But where I had sunk into a pool of frustration, cynicism, and nihilism, Joyce was overflowing with positivism and enthusiasm. It would be a confirmation of my own sourness to bluntly suppress her enthusiasm. I resolved to approach the situation in her case constructively.

We arrived at the office. I hadn't been there for a while and hoped to find a completely empty floor. With Diana in the elevator, there was little chance of that. Joyce spontaneously started talking to Diana and introduced herself as a colleague from London who had come to our office to brainstorm with the expert in the HR outsourcing domain. Diana found it difficult to conceal her surprise and shot me a scathingly derogatory look. A somewhat stiff smile was my answer. I hoped that Diana didn't feel compelled to ruin my professional reputation, and thus my chances of attracting, in about 20 seconds. God, elevators are so uncomfortable. You don't know how to stand, what to look at, what to say. At least, that was true for me, especially at that moment. Joyce had no problems. She stood talking naturally to Diana, looking at her with genuine interest and making light gestures with her hands to support the spoken words. I was sweating like an ox, staring at the ceiling and counting the seconds in my head. Diana left the elevator on the 5th floor. Luckily, no one else stepped in. We climbed further to the 8th floor, where I had reserved a room.

"You didn't know her?" Joyce asked me.

"Ooh, ooh yes, pretty good… We see each other so often that we no longer have anything to say in the elevator. Sometimes, we practice the 'elevator speech' when we have an important meeting." No further difficult comments or questions. Room 815, the only room with only one 'frosted glass' window, so there was little chance of people seeing me, was reserved.

Will, John, and Melanie, three faces I had banished to the dusty, musty back rooms of my memory, looked at me in bewilderment as I swung open the door. Will apparently anticipated a scene where the punch could come from me this time.

"John… Call the reception… Or no, call the police!" In times of panic and crisis, a great boss always remains calm, acts decisively, and gives the right instructions. The tone was set. As John furiously hammered the phone keypad and shouted, "Hello, hello…" Will stood up to keep me under control.

"Harry, stay calm, let's discuss this like adults… I thought we had talked it all out anyway."

Will's hand rested on my shoulder. If I really wanted to beat him up, this was the perfect opportunity. The plastic toy brass knuckles were missing from my pocket. The situation was ridiculous, pathetic, and amusing at the same time. However, my entire actions were driven by Joyce, with whom I wanted to spend the day, who I wanted to know, smell, taste, and feel better, so I had to get out of this unscathed.

Joyce did not fully realize the seriousness of the matter and spontaneously started introducing herself to everyone, starting with Melanie. "Joyce Doyle, London office, pleased to meet you…"

Melanie didn't know what to do, and Will had not given her a role in this scene. The two ladies started a chat on the sidelines.

"It's constantly busy. I've always said that damn reception doesn't work," John shouted.

I poked my head through the doorway into the hallway and called to reception, "Angela, can you please come over? There has been a misunderstanding here."

Will seemed somewhat distraught because I apparently did not live up to his expectations, which clearly included verbal and physical violence.

Angela rushed over. In the meantime, John had reached the local police through intelligence and now tried to explain the reason for his call.

"Angela… I think there has been a double booking of this room. It was reserved for Joyce and me, but apparently also for our friends here," I said. Angela was embarrassed, and this rarely happened to her.

"You don't think you're going to let you kick me out of a classroom, rat," Will hissed as he leaned over the table to end John's conversation. Melanie and Joyce watched this bizarre spectacle from a corner, with Joyce's beaming smile not only delighting me but also indicating that she had no idea of the prevailing mood.

"No, Will, I know my place. Angela, could you kindly arrange another room for Joyce and me."

I gestured to Joyce; she quickly shook hands with John and Will, and we disappeared with Angela.

"That was Will… The Will…?" Joyce asked enthusiastically. Yes, that was the Will. I decided not to make any insinuations, to leave out the history, my history, with Will, John, and others, and not to be tempted by lame jokes about The Willy.

Angela led us to another room, the 803, the room where we typically held video conferences and where no daylight could enter because there were no windows at all.

"I'm sorry, but this is the only room left today. Is that okay, Harry?"

"Fantastic! Thank you."

"Hey… uh, Harry," Angela began hesitantly, "Rumors are going around that you are leaving Value Creators. I guess that's pure gossip."

I laughed. "If you knew what I hear in the corridors… if we combine the gossip circuit of the secretaries with the rumor mill from the business, we get an interesting reality. I've already heard that Will's wife didn't die in an accident but committed suicide. Or that Ed didn't accidentally shoot his gun at Frank's back and that I'll have a wild affair with Joyce. Do you know Joyce? This is Joyce from our London office."

Poor Angela... She disappeared with shame on her cheeks... yet I had not lied. The door closed, and Joyce settled in. I followed her movements, the hands unzipping her laptop bag, taking out the computer, plugging in a cable, plugging it in, turning on the laptop, her body sitting down on the chair, the tight black pants that showed the contours of her buttocks as she shifted on the chair, her white blouse that stretched tight around her breasts as she bent over to plug the Internet cable into the 'hub' that stood on the table, her dark blonde hair that fell casually hanging around her face.

"We can get started. I have prepared a basic presentation that will give you the context." Our eyes met, and we kept eye contact for a moment and a few seconds. The silence was short. "...and then we can take it from there."

"I'd like to take you right now, right here," seemed too early. Concentrate Jones! I sat next to her, and we went over her presentation together. It was thorough and clear, with the right synthesis of pain points and priorities. The five centimeters between her hand and mine were not unbridgeable. Her voice and the clicking of her right index finger on the mouse put me in a kind of trance that could last forever. Unfortunately, something was also expected of me, and that was initially something intellectual. My humor and my intellect had to become the combination that would ultimately be successful, like a mathematical formula: intellect + humor = sex. The formula of love escaped me, but it was also secondary at the moment. "I still love that woman," I tried to convince myself.

Based on the principle that the end justifies the means, I focused on the case, on the problems of a Telecom company with 50,000 employees, three decentralized locations and one head office, 2 current HR systems, one an outdated in-house developed system, the other, the renowned HR Toy Software implemented 2 years ago by one of our local competitors. The implementation of HR Toy Software had proven to be a fiasco with a doubling of the budget, and still, the employee payments were incorrect. In this case, Joyce tried to make way for the complete outsourcing of their HR transactions through our outsourcing center in Budapest. The detailed business case promised ultimate savings of millions of pounds, wiping out the costs of replacing the two current systems and the losses incurred from the failed implementation of HR Toy Software. The proposal was to sell this outsourcing deal via a purely value-based contract. A beautiful story. We worked focused on the different scenarios for two hours. Joyce was very sharp and certainly smarter than me. That was what attracted me to Julie. A woman who was independent, intelligent, much smarter than me, had a sense of humor and was attractive. Hints of her perfume entered my nostrils, and her eyes were restless as she thought deeply and answered me. By noon, we had gotten through everything, as far as I was concerned. It had been a damn long time since I had made an intellectual effort like that for two straight hours, and I was satisfied because I had a strong feeling that solving this difficult quiz question had brought me a lot closer to my final goal.

"You're brilliant," Joyce told me as she closed her laptop. It had been a long time since I heard that. But who knows what fellow doctors or psychiatrists said to Julie about her qualities that I had not appreciated for centuries. Could it be that, so simple, sinking into the routine conversations of the day that were about each other's daily activities for the sake of decency? They were mainly concentrated on educational content and had little or nothing to do with the core of the relationship, the true reason for wanting to be together. The wonder, the mutual adoration, the mystery, the journey of discovery without reaching the end of the world, the mutual respect. And express all this in implicit or explicit verbal and non-verbal behavior. With Julie, all those elements were still there... but they were hardly mentioned anymore.

"You're funny..." "You're brilliant..." innocent three-word sentences may not have been consciously spoken as meaningful. But they hit like a bomb.

"What are the plans today?" I asked as neutrally as possible.

"I made an appointment with Hilde at 1:00 PM because we are together in a task force of 'young high potential women' and have to prepare an assignment. That lasts until 3:00 PM, and then I take the plane at 6:00 PM." Now I also knew who gave her my name. A task force of 'young high potential women,' how do you come up with that? Since I did not want to convey anything negative to Joyce, I did not ask any further questions, but it was clear to me that a task force with such a composition, perhaps intended to analyze the problems of this target group further in order to give them better career opportunities, was a farce. More important was to come up with an approach that would make it possible to spend longer time with Joyce. I decided to go for the shameless, direct attack.

"So you mean, that's it? We're not going to see each other again?" Direct attacks can end disastrously, which is part of the calculated risks. It was a 'when are we having sex' incognito, but it was still a clear attack, and since Joyce was smart, despite her naivety, she would give me a response that would not be misinterpreted. There was silence as she gathered all her things and put them away. My English wasn't that bad after all. Maybe I should have just said, 'Let's have sex' to avoid any misunderstandings. Why was I so interested in this woman, the mother of two children, who was the same age as Julie and I? Yes, she was a beautiful, attractive woman; she had humor, was smart, and was well-developed. What the hell was the difference with Julie? If I met them for the first time, I would most likely choose Julie without hesitation. And next to whom would I want to wake up feeling good day after day? Without a doubt, Julie... So, what the fuck?!

"There are always solutions possible; no problem is insurmountable."

For a few seconds, the relevance was lost.

"And this can hardly be called a problem... I'll just take a later flight." Her eyes sparkled when our eyes met. "I'm free from 3 PM, so you better think about the program for the rest of the day, the restaurant you're taking me to, and the excuse you're selling at home. Good luck." Few women embarrass me, but Joyce was one of them.

"Okay," I replied. In retrospect, I realized that her response had also been a test for properly interpreting the intent of my comment. She had expressed herself so bluntly because she had nothing to lose, and my response would have either clearly indicated that she had misunderstood me or confirmed what she suspected. This did not automatically mean that she had had her cards looked at herself. But with my simple 'okay,' I had exposed myself completely. All power lay with her. It was too late to change anything, and it didn't make me feel insecure as I was convinced that her desire for me was just as great. She was gone. After my 'okay,' she left. I promised Julie and the boys I would pick them up from school. Since I had told Julie about my meeting with Joyce and that I had picked her up from the airport, any excuse would be irrevocably suspect. How was I going to manage this, Julie, the children, my guilt complex, and my desire?

The rest of the day was open to me to unleash all my creativity. I saw no better way out than to confess to Julie that I had rescheduled with Joyce in the evening as we had not completed our work, and she had other appointments during the rest of the day. I decided to pick up the kids around 4:00 PM, so I had time until 6:00 PM to give them a bath and have an aperitif with Julie. I would leave Joyce a voice mail with a proposal to pick her up at the office or her hotel at 6:30 PM if she would text me the address. It would also be better not to meet her until later so as not to give the impression that 1) I had all the time in the world and 2) I was so excited to go on an adventure with her that I was eager to get started at 3:00 PM. Hilde's desk was waiting. What I still had to do was book a good restaurant where we could talk intimately enough, and the chance of meeting acquaintances would be minimal. After browsing my restaurant guide, I chose a relatively new establishment for Foucault in an old church. On the balcony, next to the impressive organ, from where the choir performed its songs in earlier times, a modular room had now been set up that could be rented by companies on certain days and, on other days, was divided into 2 or 4 small rooms; seating areas for private functions. I booked one of those 'confession rooms' as they were playfully announced on the website.

Satisfied with my strategy, I called Julie.

"Hi… I can't join you for dinner tonight. Joyce and I still have to finish a presentation, and we could not complete everything."

I deliberately left out 'unfortunately' from the first part of my sentence because it would have been about it. I tried to communicate the plans as neutrally as possible, meanwhile I tried to visualize Julie and imagine myself in her psyche.

"Okay, who's going to get the kids?" sounded without any undertone.

"I'll pick up the kids around four, then I'll be home until about six. I'll bathe them. If you get home early, we can have an aperitif," I tried.

"Oh, that's a good idea! I actually wanted to do some shopping, but that can also be done tomorrow. I have my last appointment at half past four, so I can definitely be home around five." I was on my guard because I thought I sensed enthusiasm, and I found the fact that she made no further reference to my plans with Joyce for the evening suspicious. But what else could I do than 'go along' with her?

"Is the white wine cold?" she then asked me.

"Yes, even a very good Chilean, so I will definitely open that one." Where were the questions or insinuations? At four o'clock I picked up the boys from school, both full of stories of the day's new discoveries and new conquests.

"Who are you in love with?" Sam asked Ben. My first reflex was that things move very quickly with today's youth, but suddenly, I remembered my own first crush that I had experienced between the ages of four and five. Amanda and I remembered her huge glasses perfectly.

"I'm in love with Ellen," Ben replied.

"Ellen? I thought you were in love with Susie?" Sam responded indignantly.

"But no... Ellen. I am in love with Ellen," Ben said in a raised voice. I followed the heated discussion through the rearview mirror.

"I'm sure you were in love with Susie," Sam insisted stubbornly. It became a 'well nothing,' Ellen versus Susie debate in which few substantive arguments were used. Finally, Sam seemed to give in.

"Why are you in love with Ellen and not with Susie anymore?"

"Hey, because Susie is blonde, of course."

Sam had none of that in return. For a bit... "But Susie was always blonde?"

"Yes, and Ellen is brown... completely, and her hair is black. That is much nicer." There is no accounting for taste. And tastes can change.

"And didn't Susie cry?" Sam asked enthusiastically.

"No. Susie is also no longer in love with me because I am no longer in love with her."

Voilà, love can be that simple. Some heartbreak? Some sleepless nights? What do you mean, chapped eyelids from crying? I also couldn't remember how my first amorous relationship with Amanda ended, but probably in the same innocent, painless, logical way as Ben and Susie. Why and when had that changed?

When I got home, I immediately guided the boys into the bath, washed their hair, put them in their pajamas, and played a game.

Julie arrived promptly at 5:00 PM. She flung off her cloak, threw keys on the dresser, kicked her shoes off from under her, and hugged her boys and husband, named Harry Jones. I smelled her L'eau

D'Yssee. It's been a long time since we held each other like that. Apparently, it was so long ago that Ben and Sam looked at it as if a circus act was taking place, performed by two clowns because it made them laugh calmly.

While the boys watched the Peter Pan cartoon, Julie and I lay on the sofa assessing her day, enjoying the perfect white Chilean. Then Joyce's text came through. I was startled by the squeaking sign that a new message had arrived, not so much because it came from Joyce but because the homely atmosphere was broken.

'Okay, 6:30 PM, Hotel Princess lobby. Joyce.' Julie asked no questions and continued to elaborate on her experience with 9-year-old Kim, a boy who had schizophrenia. It was 6:10 PM.

"Hey honey, I gotta go."

Gulped down the last mouthful of wine and pulled my arm out from under Julie. Still no reproachful question or look, but a feeling of guilt that demanded attention.

Why would I put on different clothes... That would definitely only be interpreted one way, especially since I was already casual, and it wasn't a logical change from costume to something easier. Still, I decided to wear a different shirt. I quickly washed, looked at my armpits, which were staring back through the stubble with glistening eyes, applied some deodorant cream, sprayed on my Aqua de Gio, and rushed down the stairs. A fleeting kiss, where two fragrances meet.

Joyce had made an effort. She looked stunning. Black leather pants (black leather pants!) above pumps, a translucent white blouse with a white top underneath and a black bra, her dark blonde locks done in a special way with small black leather clips, long silver earrings, black mascara, a line under the eyes, neutral but emphatic, painted lips, a crushing smell.

"You look fabulous," I cut straight to the point.

"Why didn't you tell me this morning?" A good sense of humor.

We had a glass of champagne in the lobby, talking about her task force and other small talk as a kind of foreplay. Then we drove to Foucault. We didn't say a word along the way but listened to Kate Bush 'Moments of Pleasure' and 'Hounds of Love.' After I announced my name, we were led upstairs. It was still quite early, so few people. The confession rooms were still empty, but we had a choice, so we went for the room closest to the organ. The concept of the confession rooms was ingeniously conceived and executed, yet it was so simple. High in the ceiling above the balcony, curtain rails of various sizes were attached in circular shapes, from which hung thick, heavy velvet curtains in various exotic shades of red, orange, yellow, and green. By closing the curtains, the 'confession room' spaces were created with tables for 2 or 4 people. No one except the operating staff had access to those areas, and the use of curtains also made them sound insulated. Joyce loved it, first the idea of a restaurant in a former church and then the concept of the 'confession rooms,' as simplistic as it was effective. The curtains closed, and suddenly, we were sitting opposite each other, completely disconnected from the world. If you had nothing to tell each other, this was the place for the painful realization. Why had I never been here with Julie?

We left each other alone while studying the menu. The background music was sublime: Jan Garbarek and The Hilliard Ensemble, 'Officium,' a combination of Gregorian chant supplemented with Jan Garbarek's sax. We finished our champagne and ordered. As a starter, we had risotto with mushrooms and truffles, then I had redfish on a bed of fresh basil with a tapenade of black olives and dried tomatoes, while Joyce went for the cod fillet with ...... We drank a delicious McGuigan Chardonnay from the Valdara's Estate in South Australia, and then another, and then another...

In fact, the entire evening meal completely escaped me. I drank the wine and ate the meal, but most of all, I felt Joyce's presence. What a woman. What made her so interesting was the combination of being a mother, humor, intelligence, and her attractiveness. And what on earth was the difference with Julie? The difference in feeling between Julie and Joyce was not so much determined by the difference in the women but was in the moment. I saw Joyce for the first time, which was accompanied by feelings of mystery, curiosity, and a sense of conquest. And I knew that if I met Julie for the first time today, I would be on fire.

"So, who is Harry Jones?" she asked me as we enjoyed the sublimely prepared risotto and well-chilled white Australian Chardonnay. A simple question asked clearly and directly. God, who was I? What was I doing? As far as I knew, it was not immediately appropriate to share that indefinitely with Joyce. She could draw the right but very wrong conclusions, and that had to be avoided at all costs. Well, who was Harry Jones? What did he want...

"Yes, I'd like to know who you are, what drives you, what turns you on, what pisses you off."

"Who do you think I am?" I simply countered. The Chardonnay drank lightly.

"I think you are searching for yourself, someone, something… And you are convinced one day you'll find it." Women, it is an unprecedented phenomenon; if they did not exist, you would never believe that someone could have invented them, but they do exist, and it is best to recognize that they have specific talents in seeing through men.

"Who am I? I am Harry Jones, a happy man who occasionally doubts his own professional choices." I wanted to keep the discussion about my private life closed and not have to answer difficult questions.

"But you are successful; everyone would envy you with your stellar career, reputation, and recognition within and outside the firm." It sounded nice and pleasant to the ears, but in terms of recognition within Value Creators Inc. Fortunately, Joyce didn't know anything yet. Let me play the midlife crisis card, I thought. So, I launched a story about a man who, at the age of 38, starts to question his vision of life, his mission, and what he has actually achieved so far. He readily elaborated on the relative superficiality of his life, the contracts, the clients, and the skepticism regarding the sincerity of his colleagues. His various alternatives were discussed, from writer to drummer and Chambre d'hôte owner to key maker. She patiently listened to all the options, the motives behind them, the feasibility of each possible avenue. Problems with armpits were deliberately omitted.

He was relaxed tonight, perhaps precisely because he was able to put his life explicitly into perspective, to clearly identify his feelings of doubt and cynicism, to calmly sort everything out and so there was no flooding going on the armpit front.

"And what is Harry Jones doing here with me on a weekday evening? What does he want from me?" she asked suddenly. Why was it about my expectations and not hers? Why was she able to position herself in the driving seat so easily? I knew what I expected from her since I met her this morning; even the why was more or less unclear to me and, therefore, actually unacceptable.

I didn't feel like having long 'beating around the bush' discussions. While waiting for dessert, we went for the crème brulée (Creem Broelee, as Joyce said); I decided to go for the direct attack so that after dessert, we would quickly end up in the bed of her hotel room or under the shower, or on the desk. My right hand slid across the table and grabbed hers while my right leg very emphatically sought contact with her left leg. The surrender was instant. But suddenly, there was a shift from first to fourth gear, and that took me by surprise again.

She stood up and bent over the table; I looked at her black push-up bra with her breasts on the edge of the abyss and tasted her hot tongue. Chardonnay with a flavor. I don't know how she did it, but suddenly, she was sitting on my lap. The French kissing continued unabated. There was an unmistakable and embarrassing fuss being made below my belt. My rod rose with such force that it almost pierced through my jeans. The question 'Would she notice, would she realize it?' had already been answered before it was asked. The zipper opened, and my sex chose freedom and was embraced by a pair of lips that were also out that evening. My eyes opened when the licking stopped abruptly. Would dessert have arrived?

Her leather pants slid over her hips, revealing her round, beautiful buttocks in a black lace thong. She stepped out of her pants without taking off her pumps. Her white blouse slid down her back, from where it fell to the floor. The white top gathered over her black thong.

"I don't know if the intention is to turn the confession room into a dark room," I stammered without too much conviction. The nipples became hard under my tongue.

The curtain slid open. I expected desert but got the shape of my own wife instead... Julie stood there and watched emotionlessly as Joyce frantically moved her palm and long fingers, with red nails, up and down my penis. The firm breasts shake to the rhythm of the powerful strokes along my trunk. Ooh, ooh, ooooooooooooh, oh God. A gigantic ejaculation followed. Yes, yes, yes, yes, yeeeeeeeeeees, yeeeeeees,...

I opened my eyes. What time would it be? My right hand felt my shorts. Why did I always lie on my stomach? Now, the bottom sheet was clearly wet. In his sleep, his arm fell on my shoulder. Damn, Ben apparently crawled into bed with us again during the night. That has been a regular phenomenon lately, always with some excuse and also at times when we were not included in having fundamental discussions about it or going through the ordeal of getting him back into his own bed. Now, here I was at 6:27 AM, with 3 minutes left before the alarm went off, and I saw an opportunity. If I went to get a wet washcloth and got Ben's pajamas a little wet, I could pretend that our son had had an accident. Time was running out. I moved carefully to the edge of the bed, trying not to make any noise, and stuck my leg outside the bed. 6:28 AM. Ben started turning, sucking his thumb, Julie stretched... My leg slid back into the bed. What now?

My hand searched through the bed for the wet spot and came across Ben's fist.

"Mommy... mommy... daddy wet the bed... I can feel it."

The light came on, Julie sat up in bed and looked at me in bewilderment. Apparently, she didn't have to verify anything; Ben's words were automatically believed as if it were the most normal thing in the world.

"Oooh, please, Harry, you should be fucking ashamed of me and your son. Does this really have to be done in front of Ben?"

"And should this discussion be in Ben's presence?" I retorted. It was indeed embarrassing, but what else could I say?

"I'm going to tell Sam that Daddy wet the bed," Ben announced excitedly, after which he left the bed.

Before Julie would reprimand me again, I took matters into my own hands.

"First of all, it is normal that you still have wet dreams as an adult, and secondly, I cannot help but think that it must always be so exuberant and tangible for us men. Maybe you have a wet dream every night."

Meanwhile, Julie had crawled out of bed to isolate herself in the bathroom. Inspector Sam, accompanied by Detective Ben, then visited the scene of the crime and cross-examined the suspect. It was clear to me that I would be the topic of conversation at school. I would best avoid contact with the teachers this week.

There was no mention of breakfast. Julie made the boys sandwiches and prepared Sam's cocoa in our new microwave while I gave them granola. Then, I helped the men with their bags and sports equipment for the internship they participated in during the holidays. At the door, they both gave Julie a kiss, and I also got a quick kiss.

"Come on, guys, let's go; otherwise, we'll be too late."

"How was your evening with Joyce yesterday?" she asked me unexpectedly.

Well, actually, I couldn't remember much. We had a nice meal and drank a lot, a lot. I couldn't even remember what time I got home or how I got to bed. Still, I didn't suffer from a hangover.

"Ooh, it all took longer than expected, but we did a good job," I heard myself say.

I closed the door behind me. I vaguely saw fragments passing by me as if in a slide projection. Red velvet curtains, a glass of cold white wine, risotto, a radiant smile, a provocative cleavage.

THE HUNTERS

We can speak of the comeback of the decade. Although The Hunters released new albums on their own label in 1998 and 2003, respectively 'Head Hunter,' a collection of obscure (concert) recordings supplemented with new material, and 'Low Profile,' an album with covers and some new songs recorded in Only two weeks in the studio of singer Josh Francis, who formed an outline of what could have been a full-fledged album, The Hunters have actually disappeared from the active music scene since 1986.

However, 'Desperate Souls' features a band that has never left, overflowing with inspiration and creativity and taking the next step towards world domination. God knows where they've been the last 20 years, but they're back. Josh Francis' voice sounds lived-in but clear, and his falsetto works wonders; James McLachlan drums with a variety that suggests there are multiple players in the game. Bassist Dave Cones is tight and rhythmic, as always, while Mel O'Connor delivers his stunning guitar performance to compete with other instruments, such as the keyboard and violin. 'Desperate Souls' is not 'Sounds of Emptiness II,' which would have been relatively easy, especially because that album is so old, but a logical successor that combines the best of what The Hunters have done in the past and where they do best. With successful reunion tours of 80s groups such as Duran Duran, the Simple Minds, and Echo & The Bunnymen on the one hand, and U2 and Depeche Mode still at the forefront of popular contemporary pop music on the other, there should also be a market for De Hunters. What have they been sitting and waiting for all this time?

Smashing Pumpkin chief and fellow resident of The Hunters, Billy Corgan said upon the release of "Mellon Collie" that the most melodic orchestrated pieces, such as 'Tonight, Tonight' and "1979," were an ode to the Hunters. In "Desperate Souls," we are reminded why, without a hint of plagiarism or repetition. Twelve new songs, all pearls, which take just under an hour and not a single second, are boring.

It is hoped that the collective musical memory has not yet forgotten the four gentlemen from Chicago or that they will at least receive sufficient airplay because 'Desperate Souls' is objectively one of the best albums of the year. Class. Concert on October 24.'

I read the article three times. My heart was beating at full speed. Who would have thought that The Hunters would return with a new album and a European tour, possibly followed by a World Tour? This called for an immediate listening session of 'Sounds of Emptiness,' their third and final release from 1986, which was cited in the article as an unprecedented masterpiece that has been the source of inspiration for many bands. I remember an article in the Voice devoted to the release of U2's Joshua Tree, which included a double interview with Brian Eno and Daniel Lanois, the producers of U2's most successful albums from 'The Unforgettable Fire' to 'All That You Can't Leave Behind,' and in that sense the creators of the Irish band's unique sound. Both expressed their admiration for the masterpiece that The Hunters had delivered. Eno, who in turn had been cited by the Hunters as a source of inspiration, compared the various songs with the 'soundscapes' that he himself had tried to shape on various albums, including "My Life in the Bush of Ghosts," of which The Carrier is still one of my absolute favorites. Eno indicated that he would like to play a role in the next album, 'The

Hunters.' Lanois claimed that "Exit," instrumentally the most sensational song of "The Joshua Tree," in which U2 tries to portray an extremely intense desolate atmosphere that neither symbolizes evil, was based on "Whatever You Say," the last song of "Sounds of Emptiness."

1986, Jesus Christ, those were the times for the music lover of the "Big sound" of the 80s. Marc and I were fans of U2, Simple Minds, Talk Talk, Joy Division, REM, and De Hunters. Every new single or album release was extensively celebrated. It was Marc who introduced me to the first CD of De Hunters, "Autumn, Fall," from 1981. I didn't know what I heard: a feeling of coming home, a feeling of perfection that had been fulfilled, a feeling of "YES!". The band made an album that was a beautiful mix of the Simple Minds' 'Sons & Fascination,' their best album and not "New Gold Dream," and Joy Division's "Closer," but with the voice of Josh Francis, who strongly resembled that of Jim Morrison of The Doors, their sound clearly stood alone. After endless touring, after 3 years, which was already an infinity in that period, the second release was released in 1984, called 'What for.' Both the European and American music press, including Rolling Stone, were extremely enthusiastic and listed the album in the top 5 of the best albums of the year.

1984 In the hot summer, Marc and I witnessed the best festival line-up and performances by our favorite bands during the annual FreeDome event in the Dome stadium. During 2 days, stiff from a combination of drinks, poor sleep on paper-thin mattresses in a damp tent, and joints, we saw concerts by the Simple Minds, who promoted "Sparkle in the Rain, U2, Talk Talk, REM, and The Hunters." Michael Stipe had sung 'Angels & Ghosts' with Josh. Now, I sometimes mused with Marc about those times and the set lists that were of an unprecedented caliber. We had all kinds of bootlegs on which pieces from those concerts could be heard, in dubious quality, but that moment never came back. In 1986, U2 was still living off the post 'Unforgettable Fire', and Live Aid successes and the Simple Minds had drifted into flat American Rock on "Once Upon a Time," "The Hunters" third and final album was released. The astonishing "Sounds of Emptiness." The cut-out review, safely tucked away behind the accompanying CD booklet, "Sounds of Emptiness," was the first album I bought on CD, speaks of a masterpiece, the standard for the 80s.' According to the same critic, 'Josh Francis is an enthusiastic and white preacher who pulls out all the stops and likes to surround himself with bombastic soundscapes and gospel choirs. The album subtly alternates emotional excesses and top-heavy piano ballads with fairly light-hearted, clear pop songs, some with a folky slant, making it a balanced gem with moments of dizzying beauty. "Sounds of Emptiness" became "Album of the Year" both on the European continent and on the other side of the 'Big Blue Ocean.' The tour was canceled before The Hunters had started the European leg, formally due to "Josh Francis" throat problems. However, there was never a sequel. It became quiet around The Hunters, and Marc and I went to university, where we paid more attention to other issues such as nightlife, the female gender, and involuntary tests and exams.

And now, as if nothing had happened, suddenly, a new album and tour. The wonders are not yet out of the world. If The Hunters could rise from their ashes with a new release, it would also be possible for Julie to regain her balance and cope with the loss of the baby. Julie had bouts of anger and frustration and uncontrollable crying fits. It was very unpredictable and tiring and made me feel powerless. I was convinced that the only means of salvation in the long term would be a new baby.

What made me most enthusiastic about The Hunters' comeback was the review of the new songs, which received no less than four and a half stars and stated that relatively new bands such as De Killers, Bravery, and Kasabian could make their mark. The album will be released in 2 weeks, while the new single "Yes, It Was Worth It" will be available for sale via Internet shops starting tomorrow and will be on disc starting next week. I was also surprised by my own ignorance of this big news, as I normally find out about new releases and tours via the Q, UNCUT, or NME.

Marc was just as excited as I was.

"Listen, we have to go to that concert at all costs. I will provide tickets and an overnight stay in a hotel because it is not near the door. Can we make it a pleasant evening?"

"Harry, that's all well and good, but I only have one leg, and I don't know how long I can last with my artificial leg. I'm slowly but surely learning to function with that thing, but I don't imagine anything yet. In fact, I can't do much more than turn on the game, straighten up, and then stand stock still. Walking is not yet possible despite the rehabilitation therapy, and I fear that hopping on that leg will still take a while."

"What does it matter?" You're not the first disabled person to go to a concert. "If we bring a wheelchair, we might get better seats." I got excited.

"Okay, let's do it, but keep in mind that you will have to drive me around and serve as my nurse."

"Deal. We can't put it past Josh to stay home!"

The tickets were expensive, €130 each, but we did have top seats. The hall, with a capacity of 10,000 people, was sold out in no time, and the comeback received a lot of positive press. Julie had always thought it was terrible music. However, I found great supporters in Ben and Sam. Every morning when I took the boys to their school, we sang along with Josh, and we formed a fantastic quartet. Rihanna and Shakira were temporarily dethroned by The Hunters in Ben's Hit Parade.

"You're really out of your mind," Julie said when I informed her that I would also be taking Ben to the concert.

"But the boy is barely 5! Harry, you can't be serious. I am calling in a justice of the peace to ban this." The weeks passed without there being a definitive answer, in my opinion, about whether or not Ben would be at the performance of The Hunters. However, extra pressure was exerted by my son, who constantly sang and hummed songs from The Hunters and announced that he wanted to be called Josh from now on. Julie accused me of manipulation. I was not aware of any harm. I only noted with pride that my son had exceptionally good taste. Sam remained fairly indifferent and sang along with everything and everyone.

Marc thought it was a good idea, in fact, an obligation, to take Ben along. He then had heated discussions with Joan, who had now moved in with Kate and with whom Marc had agreed, in anticipation of the formal divorce, to alternate the children every other week. On the evening of October 24, the children were supposed to be with Joan, and there was apparently no question of Victor or Stan being allowed to come along. Stan was not an issue at all because he was still recovering from his accident. Fortunately, the latest examinations had shown that everything would be fine again in the long term and that his speech impediment would also be temporary so that belting out songs from The Hunters would not be a problem in the future. But the party was canceled for Victor, too.

"What the hell is more harmful, do you think, a pop concert where elderly men and women experience a harmonious moment together or an evening of compulsory watching Bilitis while your mother is chatting with a strange lady?" I tried, but Marc had lost out. There would only be three of us going.

"I'm staying with Sam at Joan's. Joan has provided a babysitter, and the ladies go out. This way, I can get to know Kate." The announcement came on the morning of 24 October while we were enjoying breakfast at the table. Since our therapy, Julie and I have consciously worked on our communication to avoid misconceptions. This last-minute announcement did not seem to me to be entirely in accordance with the standard steps of a good communication plan. I also hadn't heard Julie talk about Joan in a long time. Since the news of the family dramas at Marc's, I didn't remember a moment when there had been contact between the two friends. But women are and remain unpredictable, so I was taken by surprise. We had come to an agreement about Ben a few days ago after he had a few hysterical fits because Julie refused to call him Josh, and he still hadn't gotten a positive answer about whether he could come along. The frequency of the "Mommy, why can't I go to The Hunters with Dad?" had increased to proportions that would have made Julie give in. A few clear agreements had been made between the spouses. First of all, there was no alcohol or joints whatsoever by me and Ben. The announcement that it also applied to Ben was a formality to make it seem a little less difficult for me. Furthermore, Ben had to wear earplugs during the entire concert to prevent permanent damage to his eardrums from the violence of The Hunters. Ben also wouldn't wear my T-shirt full of holes and questionable spots from 1984. Finally, I had to assure, swear on the heads of my wife and children, that I would always shake Ben's hand. Julie had come up with the idea of linking us together with a real handcuff, but when I convincingly objected that we wouldn't even get into the stadium with that and there was a good chance that we would have to spend the night in a cold cell because I was considered a potential pedophile who had kidnapped an innocent boy, she abandoned this idea.

So now the entire Jones family would travel, and halfway through the journey, my wife and Sam would join the two lesbians, then I would pick up Marc so that Ben "Josh Jones," my best friend, and I could go to the concert. Julie was about as excited and elated as Ben and I. The thought of a night out with the two lesbians apparently created a particularly good mood. The thought that Julie wanted to go out made me feel good because I saw it as proof of the recovery process she had gone through. She started to enjoy everyday things again, such as sharing her practical experiences without limits, drinking a glass of red or white wine, having sex from time to time, etc.

"Where are the ladies going tonight?" I asked along the way.

"Oh, we're first going to have a bite to eat at the Garlic Sisters and then go to a modern interactive theater piece that Joane had read good reviews about in "Sizzzzz."

"The Sizzzzzzzzzzzzzzzzzzz… What is that? A magazine for out-of-control pots?" I must admit that I expressed my subjectivity. I felt that Joan had put my best friend to shame, and somehow, I also doubted the sincerity of Joan's preference for her own sex. I had clearly sided with my friend unconditionally. On the other hand, it also bothered me that my own Julie was going to experience an intimate program with two lesbians tonight, not so much because of a fear that she would also turn out to be from the other side and that I would soon also be a single man, but mainly because I was only too happy to be a wallfly witness to everything that was going to be discussed and experienced.

"The Sizzzzz" is indeed a magazine for emancipated and feminist women, and that target group certainly includes lesbians. The play Pink Pussy received rave reviews."

"The PINK PUSSY?" I interrupted her loudly, "Don't make me laugh."They call that a theater piece. I call that a sex play Also, not very original, the Pink Pussy. The pussy, the sticky clit, the wet seam, the gray canal, the slimy slit, the drawling lip, the pouting plum, the brilliant genitals. Do you mean rock-hard porn with an interactive component? I hope you are well-shaven."

"Daddy, what's a pink pussy?" Ben asked from the backseat, who still heard surprisingly well despite the earplugs already plugged in.

"Harry, behave responsibly towards the children for once," the child psychiatrist ordered me, "those childish, adolescent comments make me sick. A pink pussy is English for a pink pussy, Ben."

"Ooh, for girls," Ben concluded.

I remained silent about it. At 3 PM, we stopped in front of Kate's, Joan's friend's house. Strangely enough, I was quick to ring the doorbell first while Julie woke Sam up and got the sleeping gear out of the car.

The door swung open, and before me stood a Black Beauty. Kate was at least as tall as me; she had beautiful, long jet-black hair, green eyes, sharp cheekbones, shiny chocolate brown skin, and a full mouth with a beautiful row of teeth, which were radiantly exposed. Although she was wearing a loose white shirt that was buttoned up to the top of the neck, I still noticed a prominent bosom. Her black trousers were tight around her beautiful bottom and long legs. Some people have all the luck, I thought. Who wouldn't fall for this woman, I wondered. Her scent was intoxicating.

"Kate, I'm Joan's friend, nice to meet you. I've heard a lot about you."

I was about to introduce myself, but before I could say a word, all the attention turned to my wife.

"Oooh, Julie, how nice that we can finally meet in person." If only it seemed that way or if I was really being pushed aside In any case, the next moment, Kate and Julie were hugging me. God damn it, I didn't see a lascivious look of love in my wife's eyes, did I? Sam rubbed his sleepy eyes, perhaps to make sure this was indeed his mother.

"Julie, could you perhaps also behave responsibly towards your own son?" I asked, slightly indignant. Joan had also come forward and kissed Julie profusely.

I don't feel right here anymore, I thought. I gave Julie a quick kiss, got in, and drove away.

"Couldn't that be a threesome tonight?" I asked Marc as I threw the wheelchair in the trunk.

"God boy, I don't know Kate spins every person around her finger, that's for sure, but honestly, I don't care. I lost my wife, and what yours is doing is not really my concern."

Marc's thoughts were with The Hunters. He had settled into the passenger seat with my help. His artificial leg lay a bit lost in the back seat next to Ben, who was in a deep sleep. I had prepared Ben for a 'Marc without a bone.' The concept of 'one leg instead of two' was clear to him, but the reason for halving the number was a lot less clear. How do you explain the word cancer to a child? There are probably proven, educationally sound scenarios for this, and Julie could certainly have helped me with that if I had asked her, but I had opted for my own variant. "Cancer is a disease." So far, so good! "Cancer is very vicious and spreads through the body to destroy everything, and to ensure that it does not eat the whole body, it must be stopped. It's like all those ants that come in in the summer and spread throughout the house looking for food." It seemed like a nice comparison that Ben would certainly understand. "And all those cancer ants have, as it were, eaten Marc's leg, and to ensure that they don't eat anymore, the doctor has removed his leg."

"And now he has a new leg that he has to learn to walk with."

"Whose leg is that?"

"That is not a real leg, but a fake leg, especially for people without bones."

"And do the ants not like that leg, or should he put powder on it so that they die?"

A discussion with a child is fantastic but also tiring because endless and a potential pitfall. Everything you say can be used against you, and even though today's kids, or at least ours, are very poor listeners, it's amazing what they remember. You will sooner or later be punished for every inconsistency.

"Don't all those ants itch?" Ben asked Marc after he woke up to the sounds of 'Hell(p)' and saw a smooth artificial leg next to him. In order not to end up in a Babylonian confusion of tongues, I decided not to wait for Marc's answer or rebuttal.

"Yes, right, Marc. Luckily, you lost that rotten leg!"

We approached the concert hall, parked the car, and looked on the GPS for the precise location of the overnight accommodation I had booked, a small family hotel, only a 15-kilometer drive from the concert.

Marc attached his artificial leg. Neither Ben nor I had ever seen an artificial leg up close, let alone the way in which such an artificial piece of plastic is attached to a real flesh-and-blood body part, so father and son stood there watching with their mouths open. Marc had already become quite skilled at it. We drove through the crowds, of course, many people in their thirties and forties, but also a striking number of young people. That made me happy. "One Hunters" hit after another blared through the speakers outside the hall. The atmosphere was electric. Posters, T-shirts, tour books, records and CDs were offered for sale in the stands in front of the entrance. Ben thought it was all fantastic, especially the black T-shirt with the gold print "Yes," it is Us. Reintroducing The Hunters on the front and all the tour dates on the back that I bought for him or actually for myself.

We passed through a special disabled entrance, where we were allowed to pass before the rest. At 6 PM, we arrived in a concert hall that was still completely empty, except for a number of physically and mentally handicapped people and their attendants. Hard to imagine that within just over 2 hours, this room would be filled to the brim, and The Hunters would be pulling their weight. The decor was extremely austere, with black cloths behind the stage, the texts 'The Hunters' and 'Desperate Souls' in gold letters, and gold-colored images of creatures that were probably supposed to represent the desperate souls. Two large video screens and a catwalk ran straight through the room almost to the other side. Gradually, the hall began to fill up. We had a fantastic seat, about 15 meters in front of the stage, which was relatively low, about 2.5 meters, I guessed. I got hot dogs and fries for the three of us while Ben stayed with Marc. I had already sinned on one of the rules I agreed with Julie. Marc drank my and his alcohol. He had clearly decided that this was going to be his night. We didn't talk much, enjoyed the atmosphere, and preferred to deal with the nerves and tensions we felt ourselves. The feeling was as intense and sincere as in 1984, which I experienced as a relief. Ben got a little impatient but quickly forgot about it when the Mexican Wave was deployed. I took him on my shoulders so that he could see it all well and see the wave roll in from far away.

The support act started at half past seven, but an unknown local band disappeared from the stage after half an hour amid loud cheering.

Eight-thirty. The lights suddenly go out. A deafening scream and whistle. The opening notes of "Whatever She Says" from the debut album "Autumn, Fall." A gigantic intro from "Mel O'Connor's" keyboard supported by the constructive pounding of James McLachlan. Then Dave Cones started unleashing his tight bass work on us, after which Josh Francis appeared out of nowhere in the middle of the walkway. The fence was off the dam. A heaving mass. Marc, Ben, and I were on another planet, and we loved it.

The set list was of an unprecedented class. Josh Francis had grown old, and in his white shirt, which hung wide open revealing a brown hairy torso decorated with a gold chain, tight jeans, and fashionable blue glasses on his pockmarked face, he, with the short spiky hair, actually looked like Jimmy Rourke. But it had to be said; the old rocker didn't cut a bad figure, was vocally supreme, and turned out to have a great voice. All well-known songs were reviewed, from the raw "Driving Fast" with a crushing solo by Mel O'Connor to the semi-acoustic "Endless Rain," in which the hall was illuminated by thousands of lighters and mobile phones. Marc loved it all as much as I did. Ben sat on my shoulders and continuously shouted Josh, Josh, Josh, And happily pounded my head with his fists.

During "Wish You Well," a cover of a song from Grant Lee Buffaloo's debut album 'Fuzzy' dedicated to the 'Best singer-songwriter and my friend Grant Lee,' Marc started to have problems with his leg, perhaps because he had been in the same position for so long.

"Do I have to pick you up?" I shouted. Marc gestured that it was OK, after which he disconnected his leg and placed it under his wheelchair in the storage net next to about ten empty plastic beer glasses. The next one was put to his lips.

"Angels & Ghosts" was the next song. I closed my eyes, squeezed Ben's fists, and thought back to 1984 and the wonderful duet between Michael Stipe and Josh Francis.

"The next song is dedicated to all of you." It's been a while, but we are happy to be back. Thanks for having bought our new record and tickets for tonight. "Thanks for having us. It's good to be back home."

The roof is off. "Young we will be," started loud roars from the audience. I watched James drum part with my mouth open. My thoughts went to my options list where, among other things, I had put drummer on. James was, if I'm not mistaken, 10 years older than me, being the oldest of The Hunters. It had to be possible to reach such a level in 10 years because although James was an absolute top drummer, two drum sessions a week for 10 years seemed to me to be sufficient to reach the same top level. But then, I didn't automatically have a band, world fame, or groupies. All in all, there weren't too many alternatives left. Value Creators had closed the door for good; Chambre d'hôte was no longer a serious option, mainly because Julie and I had decided that we wanted our boys to grow up in a city environment. Sort of for the same reason, and because I didn't want to think about missing out on my children's development, the world traveler was also eliminated.

"Young we will be. Forever young, forever young," Josh sang about 10 yards away from me. His shirt had come off, and his toned body, adorned with several enormous tattoos, glistened with sweat in the red spotlight. An absolute apotheosis. The crowd was frenzied. An artificial leg was thrown onto the stage and landed at the singer's feet. Josh picked up the leg, shrugged, grinned, and played air guitar with it for a moment. Out of the corner of my eye, I saw Marc get up; Ben went crazy on my shoulders, shouting and clapping. Marc shouted something, but I couldn't hear him; he was staggering. To my right, there was a fat woman pushing against me. His left wrist slipped from my left hand I twisted to the right again as I tried to tighten my right-hand grip above my head. The face looked vaguely familiar An ugly, bloated face. GoddammitJane. Ben slipped out of my hands and was lifted over the heads by a security guard to the stage. Marc stood up for a few seconds and suddenly started moving. One… two, three hop steps, I had lost Ben Panic struck. How could that be? "Ben, Ben," I shouted.

"Forever young, forever young, forever" sounded from thousands of people. "Take me higher, take me higher," Josh roused the audience.

The crash was huge. He hit his head against one of the crowd barriers and immediately lost consciousness. God Almighty. I pushed my way through the crowd and started dragging Marc, who had to get out of there urgently to avoid being trampled. Kicking and pushing in my back. On my knees, I crawled forward through the maze of legs. Behind me, I thought I heard a shrill female voice calling my name. The "Guards" were already there, with their dark gray suits hidden behind "Red Cross" vests. Marc was taken away on a stretcher through the narrow aisle between the crush barriers and the stage. Above me on stage, Ben was beaming, hand in hand with Josh Francis. The swirling sea howled. In the room, I think somewhere under the stage, were rows of stretchers with unconscious or overheated people. I counted 29 legs. We could follow the concert through the speakers that hung from the ceiling in two corners of the room.

"What's your name? Name you know?" "Name? I am Josh, and you, eh?" Screaming.

"Ben," I heard my son say loud and clear as applause and whistling sounded in the background. Marc was treated with ice and water. "That's my son. Someone has to go get him; otherwise, he will be lost!" I shouted.

"What's that." Consternation on stage. "You want that leg.? You want the European leg of our tour?" Hilarity rippled through the room.

"Wait, someone has a pen? Thanks. Here you go, Ben!" Mel O'Connor's screeching guitar flew through the speakers like a rocket, and James Mclachlan also resumed the rhythm of the chorus.

"He won't need it. Forever young he will be!" Josh roared for the last time, the tight beat dying away and a synthesizer transitioning into the absolute tear-jerker 'Once.'

"Damn, where's my paw?" Thank God Marc had regained consciousness, although in a terrible state.

"Dad, dad… have you seen me?"

There he stood, next to a huge security man who had come to get him, my son, proud as a peacock, with an artificial leg in his hand with 'Yours.' written in thick black marker. Forever Young. Josh' was written. I felt tears welling up.

"Of course, I saw you. Come here, buddy, you were amazing."

I embraced him and held him tightly against me. Marc admired his leg. "You did well, buddy," and he patted Ben on the head. The sound of a clapping, stamping, roaring mass. The band had gone backstage to prepare for the admissions. The wheelchair was wheeled into the room. We decided it had been nice. Ben was on cloud nine. I was mostly relieved. Marc was silent.

"Love, I'm having a great time. You? The Pink Pussycat is famous!" The text broke the silence in the car.

"Our women are enjoying themselves," I told Marc.

"Your wife is having fun with my ex and her new flame," he said dryly.

Yes, phenomenal here, too. Say hello to the Vulgar Vulva," I sent back.

Ben continued to sleep in my arms as I carried him up the stairs to our hotel room. Marc had decided to linger in the bar for a while, and the cognac had been served. It was a nice little hotel at the beginning of a forest. Ilse, a not-unattractive blonde woman of about 40, ran the business and welcomed us like a real hostess. The hotel only had five rooms, and tonight, only three were occupied. Hopefully, our hostess didn't have to do it for the money.

"Do the gentlemen want a nightcap? I'm ready for it myself." I said thank you kindly and used Ben as a valid excuse. Besides, I was tired, and my ears were still ringing. Ilse and Marc stayed behind in the bar.

Ben continued to sleep peacefully. He was probably on a stage somewhere with Josh Francis. The sheets were crystal clear and felt fresh on my body. Delicious. Sleep immediately took possession of me. A writer, a drummer, and a key maker sat at the bar, bragging about their experiences as the drinks flowed. The writer boasted about his new book, a fiction novel, which had sold 100,000 copies before its release and whose film rights had recently been sold to a major distribution house. The drummer seemed a bit old for a celebrated rock god, but the success of his group, De Master(de) Baters, was undeniable, and the attraction he exerted on the female beauty, including the bar lady, in the pub proved the opposite. The keymaker heard it all, told about an affair he had with a 25-year-old nun since he had to repair a lock in the monastery. But it wasn't all roses and moonshine for the keymaker. He had recently been called to repair a lock in a private castle. He had rang the doorbell, but no one had answered it, so he went to explore through an open back door. His call to someone went unanswered until he heard a name called on his way to the top floor. With his heart pounding in his throat, he crept toward the sound, the door standing ajar. The man sat naked on his knees in a pool of urine and feces, waving a gun in front of him. The stench was sharply pungent. "Harriette, Harriette, Harriette, Harriette," he shouted continuously as tears streamed down his cheeks. The gun in the mouth. A dull bang.

I opened my eyes. The crash was caused by Ben falling out of bed. He didn't notice anything and continued to sleep peacefully after I put him back to bed. 6:49 AM. A thin ray of light filtered through the curtains. The carefully whispering whistle increased in volume and turned into a cacophony of singing. I stared at a crack in the ceiling. It would be a big leap into the unknown, which I only dared to do because I knew Julie supported me.

IN THE ATTIC

The BMW stood gleaming in front of me as the man meticulously inspected it. Only 50,000 kilometers on the odometer. Not much for a year-and-a-half-old car. How many of those miles would have been spent touring without any purpose or destination, listening to music?

"That all looks good. We noticed a small stone chip in the windshield, but that is within the margin. If you would like to sign here for approval."

I signed for the last time on behalf of Value Creators Inc. My cell phone, laptop, and car were all returned. I was lost in life. Where were you today without a car, cell phone, or computer? Nowhere. That appealed to me as long as I didn't have to give up my Volvo Bertone and iPhone. Julie waited for me in the car and gave me a kiss after I got in.

"And, relieved?"

I laughed and took her hand in mine. "Still a bit of a sentimental moment. Not so much about leaving Value Creators, but simply because of the milestone and the end of a period."

"And you, how are you feeling? Not too much trouble?"

I believed her denial.

We drove home to the tunes of The Hunters' 'Absolution'. Even Julie sang along. As we drove into the driveway, we saw the painting company's van driving away.

"I'm going to pick up the boys; you go and see what it looks like," said Julie.

"Hmmm, I'm going to look, and I feel like I'm about to start!" We said goodbye. An excited feeling came over me.

The room was small, about 2.5 by 3.5 meters. We had to have a wall added specifically to achieve the minimum dimensions. I had bought the parquet in an antique store where they claimed that the planks had been in a church for hundreds of years. I didn't know if it was true, but it was heavily worn oak and radiated enormous wisdom to me. I had had the desk unused in the attic for a long time. It had belonged to my grandfather. A clumsy piece of furniture, a huge top, and a green leather inlay as a worktop on dark oak legs. Julie had bought the chair at a flea market. The feathers came through the velour seat cushion, which was something. A brass oil lamp provided the desk's sparse directional lighting. Furthermore, no sockets or electricity. There were candles, four in total: one on my desk, a thick red one, one on the wine cabinet, and two in the holders that were mounted on the wall next to the door. The wine cabinet was a different story; it was bought from a winegrower in the Rhône region, in Gigondas, who quit because he had no successor. The man was over 80 and was no longer able to maintain his vineyards, so he watched with dismay the quality of his red grape juice deteriorating. Gigondas is located north of Châteauneuf-du-Pape, and while the wine is clearly slightly less rich and complex than that of its famous neighbor, I prefer the Gigondas precisely because it is less heavy. We came across him more or less by chance during a trip to the area. Machotte's wine cellar was wonderfully located in a disused tunnel of the Orange-Buis-les-Baronnies railway line. That afternoon, he had decided to finally throw in the towel, and we found him in an emotional mood in his tasting room. Given the smell that hung around him, I think he had already drowned his misery. He tasted with us without spitting. I had placed two boxes of 24 bottles in my car when he motioned us to a dark corner of his tasting room. He opened a small cupboard, beautifully polished ash wood, with drawers and a door with small cut glass windows. A Gigondas Domaine de la Machotte from 1972 was opened without further questions and drank in silence by the three of us. It was an incredible wine, dark purple red with a powerful and spicy bouquet of raspberries with a slightly burning scent, which tasted full and powerful on the tongue.

"That was the last bottle from my private collection that I have here in the tasting cellar. I still had four absolute favorites left. Until this morning." He smiled, showing his toothless gums. "I started it at 11 o'clock."

He looked at his clock. In just 4 hours, the good man had outwitted four bottles. "Take my locker with you as a souvenir," he said, almost pleadingly. Although I thought it inappropriate to take advantage of a drunken old fool, he persisted and then carried the copy to my car himself. And here it was now, packed with bottles of red and white wine of a somewhat lesser caliber, which were supposed to help me through my lonely hours and perhaps provide the necessary inspiration.

We had never used the attic except for storage space. It was an immense area with many possibilities, too much for my plans. Hence, the wall I had installed. The stairs to the attic were a rickety steep slope with narrow steps.

"Shouldn't we replace that?" Julie had asked me. After much deliberation, I decided to leave it as is because it fits my idiotic image of authenticity that I was pursuing or that I had imposed on myself as a condition for success. On eBay, I found the masterpiece that would complete my working environment. I kept bidding, greatly exceeding my original budget, and eventually being able to call myself the owner for €560. As happy as a child, I announced my 'prize' at dinner. Ben and Sam had no idea what it was about, and fortunately, otherwise, they would have come up with alternatives such as a self-inflating Superman costume or a turtle that can be transformed into a fighter, all things that were much more likely to be worth an investment than my second-hand typewriter. A red original Corona & Smith from 1937, one of the first truly portable typewriters due to its ingenious four-row keyboard. Legend has it that this generation of Corona & Smith typewriters resulted in a fifty-fold increase in typewriter sales.

My exercise bike remained downstairs. Although I had doubted it for a long time, it did not match my ideal image in a certain way, so in order not to disturb that, my physical efforts were limited to the second floor. I couldn't figure out one, two, or three based on the color of the walls and ceiling. Julie had her preferences for eggplant red walls and white for the ceiling but did not really try to influence my choice. In the end, I chose a sand-colored relief paint that made the walls look old," which, despite the artificial character, gave me a good feeling, and that was what mattered. The feeling.

My little room, with its off-white ceiling and the dark brown frame of the large window overlooking the orchard, looked exactly as I had seen it in my dreams, ready to be inaugurated. The orchard was marred in the middle by a gigantic patch of ash caused by the campfire that I had organized there last weekend to symbolically burn up all my chamois shirts. We turned it into a real happening with friends and family, lots of drinks and good food. Originally, I was unsure whether I should make my mother witness this celebration because she would have a lot of trouble with the unnecessary destruction of all the textiles. Ultimately, I felt that my mother should be there because of the importance of my choice and the impact on my physical and mental health. I also invited my friends Marc and Fred and their respective supporters. In Marc's case, this meant his artificial leg, children, ex-wife, and girlfriend. Despite his situation, Marc was in reasonable shape. This again matched my friend's picture because, given all the misery he had been confronted with, he turned out to be able to deal with all those elements as if it were the most normal thing in the world and certainly not a reason for frustration and cynicism. He had relatively easily come to terms with Victor's accident, his wife's choice (and damn, Kate was still a hottie), giving up his leg, and his brutal dismissal. What else can you do? Driving through the employer's front and parking your car at the reception, killing your wife, and raping her friend, for example, were just a few spontaneous thoughts that came to mind while I sipped from my glass and inhaled the sharp burning smell. Luckily, I didn't have to think about it seriously anymore.

Fred dropped out without excuse; he just didn't feel like traveling over 900 miles to burn my shirts. A number of insignificant neighbors were also invited, not so much because I had any social intentions, but to prevent the smoke development from giving rise to angry phone calls to the police and fire brigade or to other panic reactions. So Theo and Annette showed up, an apparently happy couple in their thirties who introduced themselves as our neighbors across the street 'for the past 5 years.' Fortunately, their faces didn't tell me anything that convinced me that I had never seen them before. Although very bad at remembering names, ugly faces or bad breath stay with me forever. And since Annette turned out to have both qualities, Theo was just ugly, I was sure. That's why I found Theo's joviality, who kept calling me 'mate' and hitting my shoulder at the end of every sentence, completely out of place.

In addition to this "There is a lid for every jar" duo, Els also delighted us with a visit. Probably about 65 years old, never married, never laughed, never lived. Els was not exactly the woman you thought of as a representative of the "Rejuvenated Vagina" target group. But Els lived next door to us, and Julie sometimes saw her in the supermarket. So the human had shown up and spent a few hours smoldering fire, smoking, snacks and drinks, and vegetating with us without saying a word. To be honest, it didn't matter to me. Nothing could really ruin my good mood. There were not even a number of unknown faces, people who didn't even bother to introduce themselves to me, and it didn't bother me. I thoroughly enjoyed the wine, a beautiful full Meursault from 98, which I only served for the real in-crowd. It was a real happening, although it was unclear to many what the reason for our social gathering was and what was symbolically burned in the first place. When, under the influence of alcohol and with a certain extra symbolic value, I took off my shirt and threw it on the fire amid loud cheers from Ben, Sam, and Marc's children, the moment had come for many to drop out. Theo gave me another friendly slap on the shoulder, Annette breathed in my face, and the rest of the herd meekly left the festivities. A very successful evening for me.

I sat behind my desk, struck a match, held it against the wick of the red candle, and placed my hands on the red metal of the Corona & Smith. A bit awkwardly but still confidently, the fingers slid over the letter keys.

Name: Harry Jones

Age: 39 years

Employer: None.

Current position: Beginning Writer

Marital status: Married

Wife's name: Julie

Wife's profession: Child psychiatrist

Children: 2, Ben (5), Sam (4)

Pregnant with a third child.

www.ingramcontent.com/pod-product-compliance
Lightning Source LLC
Chambersburg PA
CBHW041305110526
44590CB00028B/4252